A House of Words
Jewish Writing, Identity, and Memory

Focusing on the way Jewish history – particularly the Holocaust – and tradition inform post-war Canadian and American Jewish literature, *A House of Words* offers innovative readings of the works of such influential writers as Saul Bellow, Leonard Cohen, Eli Mandel, Mordecai Richler, Chava Rosenfarb, Philip Roth, and Nathanael West. Norman Ravvin highlights the concerns that these disparate writers share as Jewish writers, as well as placing their work in the context of the broader traditions of multi-culturalism, post-colonial writing, and critical theory.

Arguing that Jewish North American writing is too commonly discussed as part of the mainstream, Ravvin places the writing of Bellow, Cohen, West, Mandel, Roth, and Rosenfarb within the Jewish context that their novels and poetry demand. He depicts a Jewish cultural landscape within which post-war writers contend with community and identity, with continuity and loss, and highlights the way this particular landscape is entangled with broader literary and cultural traditions. He considers Bellow and West alongside apocalyptic narratives, discusses Cohen in relation to the counter-culture, examines Mandel's postmodern view of history, and looks at autobiography and ethics in Roth and Rosenfarb.

At once scholarly and poetic, *A House of Words* will appeal to the general reader of Canadian, American, and Jewish literature and history, as well as to specialists in these fields.

NORMAN RAVVIN is an assistant professor of English at the University of New Brunswick. He is the author of the prize-winning books *Sex, Skyscrapers, and Standard Yiddish* and *Café des Westens*.

McGill-Queen's Studies in Ethnic History
SERIES ONE: Donald Harman Akenson, Editor

A House of Words

Jewish Writing, Identity, and Memory

NORMAN RAVVIN

McGill-Queen's University Press
Montreal & Kingston · London · Buffalo

© McGill-Queen's University Press 1997
ISBN 0-7735-1664-6 (cloth)
ISBN 0-7735-1665-4 (paper)

Legal deposit fourth quarter 1997
Bibliothèque nationale du Québec

Printed in Canada on acid-free paper

This book has been published with the help of a grant
from the Humanities and Social Sciences Federation of
Canada, using funds provided by the Social Sciences
and Humanities Research Council of Canada.

McGill-Queen's University Press acknowledges the
support received for its publishing program from the
Canada Council's Block Grants program.

Canadian Cataloguing in Publication Data

Ravvin, Norman, 1963–
    A house of words : Jewish writing, identity, and
    memory
    Includes bibliographical references and index.
    ISBN 0-7735-1664-5 (bound) –
    ISBN 0-7735-1665-4 (pbk.)
    1. Canadian fiction (English) – Jewish authors – History
    and criticism. 2. Canadian fiction (English) –
    20th century – History and criticism. 3. American fiction
    – Jewish authors – History and criticism. 4. American
    fiction – 20th century – History and criticism. 5. Jews in
    literature. 6. Holocaust, Jewish (1939–1945), in literature.
    I. Title.
    PR120.J48R39 1997   C813'.54098924   C97-900546-9

Typeset in Palatino 10/13
by Caractéra inc., Quebec City

To the memory of my grandmother Chaya Dina Eisenstein,
a storyteller and keeper of the record

Contents

Acknowledgments

The gathering of these essays gives me the opportunity to thank important teachers: Andrew Busza, Craig Tapping, and Henry Auster. As well, I am indebted to Richard Menkis, Teresa Heffernan, Dominic Rainsford, and Marlene Goldman, who offered me the opportunity to present some of these essays in public forums. Shelley Butler, my first and best reader, made this a stronger work through her constant advice and support.

I appreciate, as well, the support of editors who chose some of this work for publication. "Strange Presences on the Family Tree: The Unacknowledged Literary Father in Philip Roth's *The Prague Orgy*" appeared in *English Studies in Canada*, vol. 17, no. 2. "Writing around the Holocaust: Uncovering the Ethical Centre of Leonard Cohen's *Beautiful Losers*," first a contribution to the Leonard Cohen Conference (1993), was published in *Canadian Poetry*, no. 33. "Eli Mandel's Family Architecture: Building a House of Words on the Prairies" appeared in *Canadian Jewish Studies*, vol. 2. Parts of my concluding chapter were presented in *Mosaic: A Journal for the Interdisciplinary Study of Literature*, vol. 29, no. 3.

I must also acknowledge the lively, cramped hallways and classrooms of the now vanished I.L. Peretz School in Calgary, where I gained a part of my love for literature and history.

1 Giorgio de Chirico, *Piazza d'Italia* (Art Gallery of Ontario, Toronto)

2 Detail from Hieronymus Bosch, *The Garden of Earthly Delights* (Museo del Prado, Madrid)

3 Pieter Bruegel the Elder, *The Triumph of Death* (Museo del Prado, Madrid)

4   Pieter Bruegel the Elder, *Dulle Griet* (Museum Mayer van den
     Bergh, Antwerp)

A House of Words

To write means to confront an unknown face.
Edmond Jabès

Introduction:
This World and Others

Jewish writing since the Second World War has been burdened – or, one might say, inspired – by the past. Like the turn-of-the-century Yiddish writers who doubled as ethnographers and returned to the *shtetl* to capture what they feared was a dying world, novelists and poets today continue to brood over their losses, their missed opportunities, and the incongruous coincidence of their good and full lives, experienced in the shadow of so much ill fortune across the sea. We read of Philip Roth's youthful happiness in Newark, of Mordecai Richler's ribald joy in watching St Urbain Street from the front stoop, of Eli Mandel's baffled view of his ancestors' difficult career as Jewish sodbusters on the Saskatchewan prairie. Saul Bellow waxes sentimental about his childhood on Montreal's Napoleon Street, and Leonard Cohen – half mythologizing, half satirizing his austere uncles, the pillars of Westmount Jewish life – finds his youthful world so plush and secure (and ultimately disappointing) that he flees it for an itinerant bohemia, the "dismal business," as he has called it, of guitar picking. But for these writers and others it is not enough simply to depict their varied North American upbringing. Each is drawn into a kind of family romance with what Roth has called the "shadowy, cramped" world of the past (*Zuckerman Bound* 458) and is motivated by a "nostalgia for the dark intensity of events that preceded" their birth (Finkielkraut 24).

I recognize this bizarre gap between generations and the compelling urge to make the past part of a fictional present. Like Mandel's grandfather, my maternal grandfather was a *shochet*, or ritual slaughterer, a necessary figure in many Jewish communities, but in Canadian terms a rather atavistic sort of professional man, a disappearing breed. Ironically, it was my grandfather's knowledge of the laws of *shchita* that got him work in Canada and entitled him to a visa across what was, in 1935, a closed border. Between his experience of small-town Polish anti-Semitism and as a travelling rabbi and *shochet* on the Canadian prairie and mine growing up in suburban Calgary and then downtown Vancouver and Toronto, there is hardly any continuity. Family stories and photographs can barely account for this leap, in the course of three generations, from one world to the next, which is every bit as wondrous as moon travel or the discovery of an eldorado around an unfamiliar bend in the road.

There is a certain poetry to all this, a melancholy narrative. Even for the descendants of those who escaped – first-generation New Worlders like myself – there is the ever-present need for a backward glance, a tendency to take this world's measure by referring to an older one and to the stories that describe that world. Such stories present us with a portal out of our secure and often unsurprising life. Much of recent North American Jewish fiction and poetry gathers its surprising power as writers clamber up to this portal, to the borderland between the limitless future and the *alte heim*. It is through this portal that Roth looks beyond Newark and glimpses his heroes, the European writers who inspire and enliven his fiction. Bellow reaches tentatively past Napoleon Street to the death haze that hung over a Polish forest. Chava Rosenfarb writes her way out of cosmopolitan Montreal and back to her first multicultural home – Lodz, the Polish Manchester – where Jewish life was a kind of high opera of communal bickering between textile magnates, Zionist ideologues, Yiddishists, socialists, and the religious. Even Leonard Cohen, a master of the contemporary, a genius at turning pop iconography to serious ends, cannot keep the spectre of the past from haunting his most carnivalesque fiction.

But many communities in relatively new countries such as the United States and Canada can claim such divided imaginary lives. Writers from a broad range of immigrant ancestries feel that, though "born and firmly lodged in" their New World culture, they "are

always walking through doors left ajar" by the memories and stories of the "people closest to them" (Kulyk Keefer, "Mosaic" 16).
What, then, distinguishes the Jewish experience in Canada and the
United States? How can we characterize the cultural landscape that
includes the experience of life in the New World setting and memories of Europe and Holocaust, as well as paradigmatic cultural
narratives derived from an often remote, but still influential biblical
tradition? In *Landscape and Memory*, the American historian Simon
Schama describes a visit that he made to his ancestral home of
Punsk in what is now Lithuania, a visit that helps us begin to
characterize this particular cultural landscape. He arrives there
almost by chance, having made a detour along his route to view
"the great primeval forest of Bialowieza" (37). And what does
Schama find at Punsk? Not Jews, of course; and no *landsmanschaft*
has erected a monument commemorating the community's massacre
during the war. Instead, beneath a thick carpet of dandelions he
discovers the remains of gravestones. The stones are "grizzled" and
covered in "mustard-colored lichen." The Hebrew lettering on them
is "virtually obliterated," but still he imagines undertaking an exca-
vation that would reveal what lies hidden beneath the ground. "I
could have spent a day," he writes, "with a shovel and shears and
exposed an entire world, the subterranean universe of the Jews of
Punsk" (36).

So, begin here! the novelist cries, invigorated by the notion of an
entire universe hidden beneath a carpet of dandelions. But almost
as quickly as Schama raises the possibility of great uncoverings in
the shadow of the Lithuanian forest, he admits that the tombs he
has found are "sliding gently and irrevocably into their companion-
able mound ... They were becoming a geological layer" (36). There
is in this scenario a familiar post-war pathos that distinguishes
much Jewish writing since the Holocaust: the promise of recovery
among ruins, an acceptance of changes wrought by passing generations alongside a steadfast need to reincorporate – at least in the
imaginary realm – a world that has vanished, its remnants obscured
by woodland and geological loam. If the biblical prophets affirmed
this link between past and present through visionary power, and
the rabbis did so by way of midrash – by hunting for hidden and
elusive meaning in ancient texts – then our contemporary novelists
and poets have found their own methods for shuttling between a
past world and our own. To map this imaginary landscape we need

to be far-reaching in our points of reference, even a bit dilettantish in our enthusiasms.

You will find in the essays that follow an approach to contemporary novels and poetry that is eclectic, that of the *bricoleur*. I have tried to take account of traditions that were vital when my people were rabbis and small-town merchants, as well as those relevant to the postmodern moment, to choose a context that each text demands. This is where focusing on the portal, the point at which the past and the contemporary world confront each other, becomes so crucial. That portal marks the meeting place between our narratives and the history that haunts them; it represents the point of confrontation between traditional manners of thought and radical new ones. And it is at this point of confrontation that so many Jewish writers since the war have set up shop. An examination of this crossroads of past and present leads us to read Richler via Freud, Roth via Bruno Schulz, Nathanael West via Bosch and de Chirico. Anne Frank winters in the Berkshires; Hitler, the ghost of a Mohawk maiden, and a Québécois with Nietzschean pretensions confront one another on an Argentinian beachfront. These points of confluence between the contemporary world and the past reveal each writer's way of contending with continuity and loss, with identity and assimilation. They are magical, these crossing places, since it is upon such landscapes that the writer's craft makes worlds appear and disappear.

PART ONE

What Sort of Home Is the Past?

Forethought:
Building a House of Words

When writing about the Holocaust, Eli Mandel, Leonard Cohen, and Mordecai Richler place themselves under a single and fundamental constraint: they will not directly represent it. Unlike William Styron's *Sophie's Choice*, D.M. Thomas's *The White Hotel*, and the television movie *Holocaust*, the work of Mandel, Cohen, and Richler does not recreate the atmosphere of Auschwitz or the mindset of Höss or Himmler. Instead, it conveys a shock of recognition, an awareness of how deeply each author's life and art have been marked by the Holocaust, as well as the sense that neither life nor art in the West can proceed in good faith without an honest confrontation with its implications. Bypassing the intractable question of how to imagine the "unimaginable" or think the "unthinkable," their work examines how the Holocaust is *lived* by those who have survived, as well as by those who were born in comparatively peaceable times, far away from the mass graves and killing sites of Europe.

1 Eli Mandel's Family Architecture: Building a House of Words on the Prairies

It is difficult to be a "memory-tourist" on the prairies, to return to relics and ruins and examine our own lives in light of the absence and brokenness of our forebears' world (Young, *Texture* 70). The cities are new, built and rebuilt so that a minimum of history remains visible. As early as the 1940s Canadian architects bemoaned the "dead hulks" that western cities and towns had inherited from earlier generations and began the transformation of their main streets, stripping them of the venerable structures that they saw as "dull monuments" to "ignorance and sentimentality"[1] (Bernstein 12). What can the avid memory-tourist find of interest on the prairie? What places remain that are evocative of the past, and which objects resonate so richly with the lives of the dead that they have the power to shape our understanding of the present? Poet and critic Eli Mandel made his way back to the ruins of Saskatchewan and wrote what are arguably his finest poems about the Jewish ghost towns of Hirsch and Hoffer, the battered landscape called "badlands" by the locals, around Weyburn and Estevan, where he encountered not only physical ruins but the ruins of memory – in his words, "the endless treachery / that is remembering" (*Out* 19). In a collection called *Out of Place* (1977), Mandel depicts the visit he made with his wife, Ann, to the abandoned homesteads and one-street towns of his Saskatchewan youth, to the relics of an era separated from ours not so much by the passing of many years as by the brute change of our society from one that was largely rural to one that is increasingly urban. In a landscape that would read for most of us like a blank page, a sheet of brown dusty scrub, Mandel conjured the "ghostly jews / of estevan" and, stranger still, the absent Jews of the Europe that Hitler made (*Out* 13).

Western Canada is often characterized as having a "short" and "exclusively 'modern'" history, but such appraisals tend to gloss over the distinct stages of transformation that the landscape and built environment of the prairies have undergone (Pérez-Goméz 13). Over twenty years ago, in an article entitled "Time and Place in the Western Interior," John Warkentin noted how farming practices had obliterated native systems of land use, and he went on to describe how the gradual decline of many agricultural communities had brought about another "remaking of the face of the land in the prairies":

The pace of change is increasing. Examples of ordinary-seeming buildings, the ones which were most common and hence all the more important, are those we are most apt to lose.

Many kinds of rural buildings are disappearing rapidly. Churches, schools and halls, essential facilities for community activities in any farm district, were scattered through the countryside in pioneer days. Numerous structures of this type are abandoned and have fallen to ruin, because of the consolidation of social activities in villages and towns. (22, 24)

Among the once-common structures that are now largely preserved through photographs are the round barn, designed to shed snow and withstand wind; storefronts marked "Saloon"; the wooden onion-domed churches of Ukrainian farmers; and washed-out urbillboards that advertised Bull Durham, Chinook Beer, and Stanislaus Flour from the sides of barns.[2]

Mandel, interestingly enough, does not include any of these vanishing melancholy sites in the Saskatchewan poems that appear in his early collections, in increasing number in *Stony Plain* (1973), and as the focus of interest in *Out of Place*. Instead he returns repeatedly in his writing to Estevan, the city of his youth on the edge of the Souris River valley in southeastern Saskatchewan, near which the Jewish pioneering settlements of Hirsch and Hoffer struggled and eventually sank. The colonists whom Mandel encountered as a boy

at Hirsch and Hoffer came from Russia, Poland, and Romania –
most of them were shopkeepers and tradespeople in their native
towns – to pursue the promise of a life free of persecution and the
opportunity to work their own land. During the late nineteenth
century the Canadian government was eager to settle its western
territories, and 160 acres of prairie could be had for ten dollars.

As Mandel offers almost no explanation of what brought such
settlements into existence and only obliquely describes the kind of
lives that were lived there between the 1880s and the outbreak of
the Second World War, the reader might mistake the poems in *Out
of Place* for surrealist experiments, wild impositions of Chagall's
Vitebsk onto the glyph-marked banks of the Souris River. In "near
Hirsch a Jewish cemetery" Mandel writes, "the Hebrew puzzles me /
the wind moving the grass / over the still houses of the dead" (20).
In "slaughterhouse"

> grandfather leading me back to the kitchen
> the farm unpainted weathered grandmother
> milking guts of shit for skins and kishke
> it's not a place for boys she says
> her face redder than strawberries
> her hands like cream (22)

Mandel's juxtaposition of worlds must read like a fantasy, a day-
dream, to anyone without memories of such scenes, to anyone who
has not stumbled onto their ruins. And in fact, he does not hide his
urge to play with this unusual juxtaposition of prairie landscape
and Jewish culture, to come up with his own fiction using the facts
at hand. Included in *Out of Place* is a letter he received from a citizen
of Weyburn, a town near Hirsch and Estevan, which takes him to
task for his reliance on poetic licence. The letter reads:

Dear Professor Mandel,

Heard you on "This Country in the Morning" and was more than surprised when you mentioned that your new book on Poetry and Prose will
be about the ghost Jewish Colony of Hoffer (or Sonnenfeld Colony which
is the correct name).

Whereas my husband and I were both born in the colony and are still
carrying on farming operations there and have a great interest in that area
we were wondering where you got your information.

It was interesting to hear you say that your wife has been out taking pictures. Would it be possible to know of this, and when and where do you plan to have your book published. We would like to buy it when it becomes available.

Thank you.

Yours Truly.

Mrs. N. Feldman (36)

It is difficult to judge if the tone of these three neat paragraphs is sarcastic, a dismissal of Mandel's version of history as a sloppy fiction, or if it is simply searching, open to all possibilities. In his poetic response to Mrs Feldman's letter Mandel admits that his own imagined sense of the landscape had "disappeared" those still living on it:

> Mrs. Feldman
> I say to myself softly
> I can't see you in the picture
> there is no one there. (37)

Mrs Feldman is, in a sense, one of the survivors who did not fit into the fiction that he derived from the absence and total abandonment he found on the Saskatchewan prairie.

In an essay discussing his poem "On the 25th Anniversary of the Liberation of Auschwitz," Mandel makes a striking connection between his struggle to develop a poetics appropriate to writing about his prairie past and the challenge of writing about the Holocaust:

The place of death, Europe and the Jews, I had identified as tradition, fathers, all that named me, connected me with the past, the prophetic, Hebraic, Judaic sense – in its alien and tragic sense not in its ethical and legalistic aspects. If the camps recorded death, it was that death I had to record, an attempt too horrible to contemplate. But the possibility of re-enacting that death began at the same time to occupy me. Its substitution, the graves of the war dead, in Europe, for example, the place of the Jewish dead on the prairies. ("Auschwitz" 216–7)

Without making any explicit reference to this "substitution" in *Out of Place*, Mandel intimates that there is an uncanny doubleness between the alien European deaths "too horrible to contemplate"

and those of his forebears on the prairies: the unlikelihood of a
Jewish pioneer by the Souris River mirrors the unlikelihood of
meeting a Jew today in Cracow or in Munich; European towns and
countrysides emptied of Jews are the tragic double of the abandoned townsites at Hirsch and Hoffer. The "town lives," Mandel
writes of Estevan, and "in its syntax we are ghosts" (*Out* 14). Just
as memory-tourists visit the sites of death camps to view the ruins
of an architecture of death, Mandel finds at Hirsch and Hoffer far
more benign, but equally mouldering ruins.

In his earlier collection *Stony Plain*, Mandel points to the similar
identity and world-view shared by those who perished in Europe
and his own forebears on the prairies. But he does so in order to
evoke the vast difference between their respective fates:

> and father knew father
> mothering the last of the jews
> who in the Hirsch land
> put in new seed
> and new codes
> and new aunts
>
> so we survived
> but had become
> being as
> we were
>
> solutions
>
> the seed
>
> the new seed
>
> final solution ("Earthworms" 54–5)

The Holocaust exists as an after-image of the Mandels' survival on
the prairies, the two experiences like opposite ends of an hourglass,
flaring away from each other but still inextricably connected. This
doubleness that exists between two vastly different vanished Jewish
worlds lends Mandel's ruminations on the ruins of Saskatchewan
a deeper resonance.

In his effort to tell the stories of the Jews of Hirsch and Hoffer – stories that he calls "heroic" – Mandel must return to the ruins of these places as well as to the ruins of his own memories (*Out* 75). At the townsites themselves he finds relics: seed catalogues, "machinery bills," "clapboard buildings," "quebec heaters," iron bedsteads (*Out* 38), recollections of "wild strawberries cocoa-butter" – what he refers to as the "taste of Hirsch" (23). In *Out of Place* his poems are juxtaposed with Ann Mandel's photographs of the southern Saskatchewan landscape. In black and white the storefronts and prairie roads of Bienfait and Hirsch look like vacant film sets, peopleless under a sky so clear and vast that the galaxy seems to have been emptied of all its heavenly bodies. Abandoned frame buildings are shot through with sun and the brilliant still air. But Eli Mandel himself undercuts any sense that these stills provide proof that Ann's vision of the landscape, her account of relics and recollection, reveals the truth. The photographs are anything but sure representations, he says: "we take the photographs to be the reality. But they're not, they're only photographs. They're interpretations" ("Interview" 87). So how much *less* reliable memory must be. In "lines for an imaginary cenotaph" Mandel erects a monument that serves as his own interpretation of the landscape:

> george hollingdale
> bruce carey
> george chapman
> jacob barney mandel
>
> William Tell Mandel: sd
> Capt A.W. (ab) Hardy
>
> Isaac Berner
>   Annie's
> son
>
> all the kinds of war
> we say our kaddish for
>
> chief Dan Kennedy
> singing
> beneath the petroglyphs

hoodoos we sd
at Roch Percée

Assiniboine songs (*Out* 30)

But the poet is quick to point out the blind spots in his own interpretation. With the rush of years and his inability to read the landscape and its ruins confidently, he admits that he must inevitably lose contact with the past. Standing before the glyphs in the badlands left by the Assiniboine, Mandel asks, "do they mean anything?" (*Out* 34) In the same way, disinterested travellers fly by on the highway beside the Jewish cemetery at Hirsch; "no one there," he writes, "casts a glance at the stone trees / the unliving forest of Hebrew graves" (*Out* 20). What you not know, quite simply, is not there, in or out of place.

Architecture in the city means hope; it means home building. Its practitioners erect structures evocative of the stories of progress and prosperity that every community needs to hear to believe in its own strength and good sense. In Canada, Calgary and Toronto have most wholeheartedly embraced the tower. Our skyscraping needles strive to counter the legendary fiasco at the Tower of Babel; with their tops in the clouds they are unfettered by heavenly decree, much less by concerns over usefulness or expense. These buildings assert a narrative at once archetypal and modern, with all relics of the past and the stories they might convey removed from sight. But on the prairies, in the wild places abandoned by their short-lived communities, the human art of architecture is reversed by the weather. Windows turn in on themselves, roofs furrow and fall, fence posts and corner beams bed down, softened to termite dust and mulch. Buildings are slowly unmade as the world reverts to form, or formlessness.

One might assume, then, that Mandel returned to Hirsch and Hoffer to undo this process of transformation and obliteration, that he wrote with the reassuring hope that his poems would "reconstruct the original artefact ... by returning to the scene of it" (Harbison 108), and that through his poems he would erect a monument to all the dead Mandels and Berners of Saskatchewan, a "version of history calling itself permanent and ever-lasting" (Young, *Texture* 4). But the outcome of *Out of Place* could not be more contrary to this urge. Mandel goes to great lengths to leave documented history *out* of his poems. He fashions instead an almost purely personal and imaginative meditation on prairie ruins. Omitted from *Out of Place* is any background information on the colonies themselves. The development of Jewish farm settlements at Hirsch, Hoffer, Moosomin, Wapella, and Lipton, as well as at sites scattered across Manitoba and Alberta, has been documented by Jewish community leaders, historians, and parliamentarians alike. John A. Macdonald and his high commissioner in London, Alexander Galt, had low expectations of the Jewish newcomers who applied through their co-religionists in Montreal for land titles in the west. They will "at once go in for peddling and politics," Macdonald wrote to Galt in 1882 (Arnold, "Jewish Immigration" 86). Galt, however, believed that by taking an interest in the Jews who were willing to homestead in the wilds of the prairies he might promote greater awareness of Canada among the famous Jewish philanthropists of Europe (Arnold, "Jewish Immigration" 93). He had in fact tried to interest the German-born Baron Maurice de Hirsch in investing in the Canadian Pacific Railway, having heard of Hirsch's success at developing and running the railway linking Constantinople and Europe ("Hirsch").

Nothing came of this attempt, but it was the philanthropic efforts of Baron de Hirsch that allowed the first Jewish settlers to go west in numbers, and through his support of the Montreal office of the Jewish Colonization Association, families continued to join established colonies. Settlements like those founded in Canada sprung up, with the baron's support, in Palestine, Brazil, Argentina, Oregon, South Dakota, and New Jersey. In 1929 the *Encyclopedia Britannica* referred to Hirsch's Jewish Colonization Association as "probably the greatest charitable trust in the world" (*Worldwide* [3]).

Although Mandel conjures up his relatives' life on the prairies in *Out of Place*, he does not claim for his forebears the central role that they played in the history of the Hirsch settlement. His grandfather, Marcus Berner, was the rabbi and *shochet* at Hirsch for thirty-two years, marrying and burying two generations of pioneers. The synagogue in which he taught and led services was the first such building erected in Saskatchewan (Leonoff 34). Berner was also an established farmer, a chairman of the school board, and a municipal councillor. Among the intermediaries who connected the colonists at Hirsch with their often snobbish benefactors at the Baron de Hirsch Institute in Montreal was Lazarus Cohen, the grandfather of Leonard Cohen, a literary peer whose career Mandel followed with great interest. Lazarus Cohen, a lumber and coal merchant in

Montreal, spent five weeks at the colony, working and studying with the settlers.[3]

Mandel positions the poems in *Out of Place* almost entirely outside this rich history, recounting none of it. Rather than turn to communal history, he includes, almost perversely, a footnote more relevant to literary than to Jewish historical archives. Instead of mining the rich stories concerning Israel Hoffer, the patriarch who gave his name to the colony he led, Mandel notes that Hoffer's son Abraham is mentioned in Aldous Huxley's *The Doors of Perception* and *Heaven and Hell*: "A psychiatrist, Abraham Hoffer has done pioneer work in the uses of lysergic acid as a means of exploring the nature and causes of schizophrenia and alcoholism. His father was a wheat farmer" (*Out* 15n).

This urge to avoid recounting documented events, to present instead a portrait of personal encounter with the memories conjured by a visit to the Hirsch area, accounts for the treatment in *Out of Place* of the old Hoffer community "vault." There is no precise description in the book of what it is that Eli and Ann Mandel discover in a vault they visit on what was the Hoffer family farm near Estevan. It is said to contain documents and artefacts of the history of the Jewish prairie settlements. The vault's floor is "littered with prairie," and Mandel recounts how he began "to feel gloomy" as soon as the discourse of "family lines," of the "census" and "newspapers," began to intrude on his own recollections and vision of the landscape (*Out* 38).[4] One critic has argued, "Writing, the subject and matter of *Out of Place*, finds it[s] first configuration in the image of the vault" (Kamboureli 270). Yet surprisingly little is read out of this configuration. The archive is a mess, a disappointment that brings on the poet's gloomy mood. In Ann Mandel's preface to *Out of Place* she describes herself and Eli as two memory-tourists who used pages "for mattresses, sheets, and head rests. When we decided a page was insignificant for our purposes or saw it was blank we placed it in a pile to use for wiping ourselves or for after love. Others became serviettes, sunshades, etc." (i).

This extravagant image of the archivists actually *making use* of history, bringing it up to date by including it in their daily lives, offers the most explicit condemnation in *Out of Place* of the urge to represent "any version of history calling itself permanent and everlasting," the kind that is presented through a monument or museum exhibit (Young, *Texture* 4). To quote James Young, whose recent book *The Texture of Memory* examines Holocaust memorials, Mandel would have us see that sites of historical importance and communal experience need not assume the "polished, finished veneer of a death mask, unreflective of current memory, unresponsive to contemporary issues" (14). Ann and Eli Mandel live in the vault, eat and make love on top of what it contains. For them the prairie ruins are ripe with history, bearing the traces of the "ghostly jews / of estevan" (*Out* 13).

By forcing us to meditate on the absence and brokenness of the vanished lives of Hirsch and Hoffer, the poems and photographs in *Out of Place* enliven the landscape and repeople the empty prairie. The "magic of ruins persists," Young tells us, in "a near mystical fascination with sites seemingly charged with the aura of past events, as if the molecules of the sites still vibrated with the memory of their history"[5] (*Texture* 119). Such sites of memory "begin to assume lives of their own" (120). And so it is with the landscape surrounding Estevan. In "the return" Mandel writes,

> my father appears
> my mother appears
> saying no words
> troubled (*Out* 13)

And for Mandel absence provides as sure a marking on the landscape as presence:

> I read the land for records now
>
> wild strawberries cocoa-butter
> taste of Hirsch
>   bags of curdling
> warm spent streams
>
> tested on the hair of berner's beard
> the ritual slaughter knife
>
> even the blood has disappeared (*Out* 23)

Within the gates of the cemetery at Hirsch, where the dead were brought from the surrounding communities, he describes himself standing "arms outstretched / as if waiting for someone" (*Out* 20). Even in a dead graveyard the past threatens to send an emissary.

Mandel's approach to history and forms of memory jibes nicely with what might be termed a postmodern suspicion of any effort at freezing the past like a death mask, at preserving an official record of events.[6] It is this suspicion that has led contemporary architects to reject what they judge to be the exhausted forms of their predecessors: nineteenth-century historical façades bearing tableaux of national and mythic heroes; and the neoclassicism exemplified by public buildings whose style, borrowed from Revolutionary France and ancient Greece, promotes "the ideal of universal laws ... science, art, government and justice" (Muschamp 30). After the shock of this century's killing fields these public myths no longer thrill us, and architects have begun to find inspiration for their buildings in "narratives which resonate with the history of a specific place" (Shubert 44) and which derive their inspiration from "personal stories grounded in life" (Pérez-Gómez 14). In the words of Vancouver architect Richard Henriquez, such work situates "the individual in a perceived historical continuum ... which includes both the built and the natural world, real and fictional pasts, and allows members of the community to project their lives into the future"[7] (qtd. in Shubert 44).

Within this historical continuum, ruins and relics can very well be built into a new building, as a structure is made to take into account its site and the buildings that preceded it there, as well as its relationship to geology and native culture. In *Out of Place* Eli Mandel finds inspiration in a similar historical continuum. He reads the landscape for the leavings of the Jews, of the Assiniboine, even of the identity-less parade of travellers who roar by in their cars, and he devises from all this a portrait of intricate depth and particularity, a scaffolding of story and image supported by ruins.

For Mandel, it would seem, the richest site for the memory-tourist is an accidental one, rather than a deliberately cared-for monument; it is one that is overgrown and infested, rather than one that politely offers an officially sanctioned commemoration. There is no rhetoric in *Out of Place* pronouncing on the absence of official signs to mark the history of Jewish settlement in the area. Mandel makes no rancorous request that his ancestors' first home in Canada be better preserved.[8] In what appears at first to be an enigmatic utterance – "no one has the right to memories" – he affirms the rightness of ruin, the need to let the land sweep back over failure and abandonment, to let it take back its ghosts (*Out* 27).

2 Writing around the Holocaust: Uncovering the Ethical Centre of Leonard Cohen's *Beautiful Losers*

Leonard Cohen's novel *Beautiful Losers* has been described as an exemplary evocation of the drug-inspired pop culture of the sixties, as a metafictional experiment in which the author self-consciously comments on "the acts of writing and reading the text itself" (Hutcheon 26), and as an example of the "New Western," a genre bent on exploring the myths of native culture while ridding the Americas of the exhausted legacy of Christianity and Enlightenment thought (Fiedler 165, 175, 185). With such emphasis, critics have sanitized the book and robbed it of its most incendiary and trenchant critique. The interpretations that have limited our reading of *Beautiful Losers* have almost uniformly ignored the section portraying a rather sordid encounter with Hitler. If we give this section its due weight, Cohen's novel can be seen as a provocative examination of the role of the Holocaust in contemporary culture and as a call to heed the lessons of the Nazi attempt to exterminate the Jews.

This demand that we read *Beautiful Losers* as a book about Jewishness may seem perverse in light of the novel's exclusion of virtually all Jewish images and thematics. In the mid-sixties, when Cohen went to the island of Hydra on a Canada Council grant with a history of Catherine Tekakwitha, the work that developed as a result of this self-imposed exile proved to be a departure from the poetry and fiction that he had published to date. Gone in *Beautiful Losers* is Cohen's masterful and lyrical use of biblical and Chassidic legends, which make up much of the allusive material in his early poetry. Gone as well are the issues so central to *The Favourite Game*: the predicament of growing up Jewish in Montreal, the heritage of a European background, the influential (and oppressive) presence of uncles who "presided over most of the institutions" of Jewish Montreal and who would have their heir become a garment man and not a vagabond poet (*Favourite* 11). Gone, in fact, except for one satiric reference at the end of *Beautiful Losers*, is the milieu of Jewish Montreal, to be replaced by the ethos of Québécois nationalism and a fascination with a kind of Nietzschean self-realization. And although suffering – in both personal and communal terms – is a central concern in the novel, it is figured, not through the prism of Jewish history, but through the dismal history of the A——s, a Mohawk tribe so lacking in good fortune that their name was "the word for corpse in the language of all the neighboring tribes" (5). Yet near the end of *Beautiful Losers*, Cohen makes a more prolonged and startling use of the Holocaust than any appearing in his writings. We must therefore ask why, in a book devoid of any explicit probing of Jewish history and thought, a book said to be a paean to the exalted, but ultimately failed, yearnings of the 1960s, does there appear the most blatant use of the Holocaust in the writer's art?

Hitler makes his appearance near the novel's conclusion, when Edith, the narrator's wife, and her mentor, F., journey to Argentina for what F. ominously calls "a little sun and experiments" (175). In the guise of a hotel waiter, Hitler enters their room with a pass-key and maintains a masterly position as he administers to F.'s and Edith's sexual yearning by way of certain unmentionable "sordid exciting commands." F. admits that he and Edith remained suppliant before their visitor, even when he "made" them "kiss the whip" (194). Hitler concludes this bizarre scene by drying their "parts" and pronouncing, with brutal deadpan irony, "I had millions of these at my disposal" (194).

Critics discuss the ensuing action without making much of Hitler's part in the narrative. Linda Hutcheon, in *Leonard Cohen and His Works*, notes a number of scattered references related to the Holocaust. Prominent among these is F.'s description of Catherine Tekakwitha's acts of self-mortification: "you know what pain looks like, that kind of pain, you've been inside newsreel Belsen" (Cohen, *Beautiful* 207). This idiosyncratic analogy represents for Hutcheon

F.'s veneration of the movie palace as a source of "vicarious experience" offering "the possibility of understanding things one cannot know personally" (19). She quotes as well from the dejected confession that F. makes before he describes the encounter with Hitler. But as with the allusion to Belsen, she does not pursue the question of why this death-camp imagery suddenly irrupts into Cohen's narrative (29).

The importance of Hutcheon's reading of *Beautiful Losers* for other critics can been seen in Sylvia Söderlind's approach to the novel in *Margin/Alias: Language and Colonization in Canadian and Québécois Fiction* (1991). Söderlind begins her chapter on Cohen by admitting her indebtedness to Hutcheon's regard for *Beautiful Losers* as "*the* quintessential Canadian postmodern novel*" (41). She makes much of the book's "insistent use of pornography" and its focus on a bizarre blend of cruelty and sexuality (43), yet she does not mention the Hitlerian fantasy of sex and violence that F. and Edith share:

– Stand up, F. Get your mouth off me. I'm pretending that you are someone else.
– Who?
– The waiter.
– Which one? I demanded.
– With the mustache and the raincoat.
– I thought so, I thought so.
– You noticed him, too, didn't you, F.?
– Yes. (177)

Söderlind is even more careful than Hutcheon to avoid invoking this interchange. She transcribes Edith's well-known utterance after the scene with Hitler, which, when translated from Greek, means "I am Isis, born of all things, both what is and what shall be, and no mortal has ever lifted my robe" (Söderlind 66). Edith's sudden transformation into a figure embodying both Isis and Catherine Tekakwitha is often seen as the novel's climactic sign that magic is afoot, that an alternative ontology is being affirmed. But Söderlind neglects to mention that Edith's claim of sacred transcendence is made immediately after the orgy that F. and Edith take part in with Hitler, which is followed by a bath using soap "derived from melted human flesh" (Cohen, *Beautiful* 194).

Margaret Atwood's early, but influential *Survival* may well have set the stage for this curious avoidance of Hitler's presence in the novel. Her thematic criticism generalizes and, I would say, trivializes Cohen's intentions by arguing that "*Beautiful Losers* depicts not only the sufferings of the victim, but the mentality of the Canadian onlooker who needs to identify with victims" (100). Stephen Scobie echoes this notion in his *Leonard Cohen*, though he admits to a certain discomfort with reading "the whole of *Beautiful Losers* as ... an allegory of Canadian society" (113). Still, he too writes *around* the encounter with Hitler, though he does mention it, calling it "the novel's most extreme sexual scene" (107) and "an outrageous parody of all the conventions of 'the orgy'" (109). Scobie draws no direct conclusions about Cohen's use of Holocaust imagery, but concentrates instead on how the section develops such themes as sexual exploration and transcendence (110). Michael Ondaatje's overview of Cohen's work leaves a similar impression, letting Hitler's "guest appearance as an Argentinean waiter [who] baptises F. and Edith with human soap" stand as one of the novel's many evocations of a "wild new cult" (53).

Just as they are consistent in their avoidance of extended consideration of the encounter with Hitler, so critics tend to be in agreement that *Beautiful Losers* is a novel that portrays the urge to transcend the suffering of secular existence by way of a rather contradictory mixture of sexual excess, self-denial, and a taboo-bending recreation of religious experience through rites both sacred and profane. Söderlind points to the characters' pursuit of the "pan-orgasmic body" as part of the need to "escape from a language of reason, history, and science into one of desire, magic, and the body, by means of which 'we are part of a necklace of incomparable beauty and unmeaning,' tending toward the dissolution of identity and the fusion of bodies" (51). Hutcheon is less emphatic about this process being the novel's guiding theme, but she does argue that the characters "are all reborn, transformed, merged together" under the guise of a "new, modern religion" of sexuality, the sacred texts of which are comic books, popular songs, and movies (18–19). Dennis Lee goes even further in *Savage Fields*, suggesting that these pop icons furnish "an arcane system of guidance" (68–9) that leads the narrator toward "psychological liberation, a religious conversion, and a reconstruction of our civilisation's way of being human" (80).

F. – the novel's embodiment of that unlikeliest of personas, the Canadian *Übermensch* – is the maestro behind all this "mystical shit," as the narrator dubs it in a fit of jealous anger (8). F. is a kind of puppetmaster, a guide and lover who uses both lies and brutally honest confrontation to force Edith and the narrator closer to an understanding of the nature of being, or what F. calls "ordinary eternal machinery" (35). His desire for clarity and power takes him to Ottawa, where he sits as a member of Parliament and dreams of bringing to fruition "the vastest dream of [his] generation ... to be a magician" (175).

As the novel progresses, F. falls more and more into the role of a philosopher-king who knows all too well that his vision is a corrupt failure. As he looks back over his efforts at teaching Edith and the narrator to "embody the best" of his "longings," he admits, "I didn't suspect the pettiness of my dream" (164, 175). It is the weight of this self-knowledge, and the ironic outlook that his failure imposes on him, which leads him to toss off irresponsible bons mots under the guise of high seriousness: he "loved the red chairs" in the House of Commons, he says, and "cherished the fucks under the monument" (174). And in an outburst reminiscent of the Futurists and their celebration of power and violence, he intones, "History has shown us how men love to muse and loaf and make love in places formerly the scene of much violent activity" (45).

F. acknowledges the failure of his pursuit of spiritual and sexual release most directly in his "Long Letter" describing his "Argentine vacation hotel week-end shack-up with Edith" (175). Here he addresses the narrator as his "Dear Friend" (170) and promises, "I am going to set you straight on everything" (173). Speaking as a decadent and world-weary cynic, F. admits that action and honest engagement with political violence have always been beyond him:

I will confess that I never saw the Québec Revolution clearly, even at the time of my parliamentary disgrace. I simply refused to support the War, not because I was French, or a pacifist (which of course I'm not), but because I was tired. I knew what they were doing to the Gypsies, I had a whiff of Zyklon B, but I was very, very tired. Do you remember the world at that time? ... In perfect sleep we took the soap and waited for the showers. (173–4)

Here the spectre of the Holocaust intrudes on F.'s account of his hopped-up claims for self-assertion and social and spiritual experimentation. He views his own commitment to politics and social transformation as a fraud, and as a kind of representative man, he speaks for a generation of beaten victims, ready to accept the most hideous and demeaning of deaths.

F. and Edith travel to the Argentine in a last-ditch effort to complete (or undo) the effects of F.'s spiritual and sexual training, what he calls his "Pygmalion tampering" (195). Pursuing the "pan-orgasmic body, [an] erogenous zone over the whole flesh envelope," Edith has found herself cursed with a body in "trouble … it kept changing sizes, she even feared that it might be dying" (175). She blames F., her mentor, for her experimentation with excess: "You've meddled, F. You've gone against God … You wanted me to go all the way. Now I'm no good to anyone and I'll try anything" (176–7).

These words are more striking and meaningful to me than the much-cited vatic impersonation of Isis, for "I'll try anything" is prescient of the threat of self-abnegation and spiritual defeat that lurks for F. and Edith behind the soon-to-be-heard "professional knock" on the hotel room's "blond door" (193). Behind the door, which itself seems to be complicit in some prevalent Aryanized vision, stands the Hitler of pornographic movies and trash novels, both of which draw on the Nazi ethos as a paradigm for images of domination and enslavement. Dressed as a kind of sadistic flasher, Hitler wears "the old raincoat and mustache, but underneath he was perfectly nude. We turned toward him" (193). This attitude of supplication, even veneration, is F.'s and Edith's automatic response to their visitor. Even more startling is F.'s nonchalant acknowledgment that "What followed was old hat. I have no intention of adding to any pain which might be remaindered to you, by a minute description of the excesses we performed with him. Lest you should worry for us, let me say that we had, indeed, been well prepared, and we hardly cared to resist his sordid exciting commands, even when he made us kiss the whip" (194).

This achievement of sexual release through violence is reminiscent of an earlier scene in which F. tries to "cure" Edith's bodily "trouble" through a gruesome description of the brutal methods used by the Iroquois to torture their Jesuit captives, bringing Edith close to the "blind realm … of pleasure beyond pleasure." Referring only ambiguously to the significance of finding such images of violence arousing, F. remarks, "Of course, the implications of her pleasure are enormous" (191).

His account of the orgy with Hitler seems to offer an acknowledgment that Nazi processes of degradation and enslavement have become not only acceptable but exciting to the popular imagination. Cohen is playing with fire here, but there is a provocation in his stance that the reader must not miss. With all pious notions of goodness dispensed with, alongside the insistence that victimization has become "old hat," though still exciting, he presents a moral predicament that touches us all. Self-denial and self-mortification – so central to Catherine Tekakwitha's, Edith's, and the narrator's spiritual progress – are seen to be part of larger projects of dehumanization through submission and surrender. F. and Edith demean themselves before the man in "the old raincoat" (193), just as Catherine Tekakwitha sacrificed herself for the faith of the "Robes-Noires" (84). Catherine's "use" as a martyr following her death is not unrelated to the "usefulness" of humans, who can be melted down to produce soap.[1] In both cases a system – be it a religious orthodoxy or an ideological tyranny – turns humans into the vital *material* by which that system justifies its own existence.

There is certainly reason to challenge this kind of reading for the way that it relativizes historical events of suffering and their particular implications. Dennis Lee notices the similarities – calling them patterns of coincidence – between "Catherine's assault on her own body" and the sadomasochistic acts that F. and Edith indulge in their hotel room. "Indeed, with its welter of flagellants the Indian village looked like 'a Nazi medical experiment,' while the workout with the Vibrator left Edith and F. 'well prepared' to bathe in human soap. Traditional asceticism and the cult of ecstatic sex are alike in the sinister appetites they release" (88). In this kind of historical free association the Holocaust exists not as a particular event to be limned, but simply as a handy metaphor for other kinds of extremity and human suffering. Such figurative use of the events of the Holocaust tells us nothing about them, but instead obscures and diminishes the distinctive horrors visited on the Jews of Europe by the Nazis. There can be no doubt that Cohen leaves himself open to such criticism by alluding to the Holocaust almost casually, in a tone routinely offhanded and ennui-ridden.

But the novel's ultimate effect is not an equation of victimhood at the hands of the Nazis with victimization by Jesuit-led colonization and, finally, with the suffering and surrender that the spiritual adept imposes on himself or herself. The Holocaust makes too shadowy and abrupt an appearance in the book to take on such thematic symmetry with Cohen's other concerns. In fact, the spectres of Hitler and Belsen are repressed as a major motif in much of *Beautiful Losers* and irrupt suddenly in allusions to gas chambers (188–9), to Zyklon B (173), and to Nazi medical experiments (209).

The scene with Hitler is avoided by most critics, I think, because it is a site of rupture in the novel: at this point all the motifs of metamorphosis, sexual ecstasy, and transcendent yearning are obliterated by the premonition shared by F. and Edith of their own deaths. Immediately before Hitler's entrance, the two friends and lovers bemoan the failure of their sexual and spiritual odyssey as they gaze out at a landscape that seems to resonate with this uncanny premonition: "A great sadness overtook us as we looked out over the miles of sea, an egoless sadness that we did not own or claim. Here and there the restless water kept an image of the shattered moon. We said good-by to you old lover" (193). F. acknowledges, as he writes of this goodbye scene, that he and Edith realized they had gone over a precipice, crossing into territory from which they would not return: "We did not know when or how the parting would be completed, but it began at that moment" (193). These doom-shrouded thoughts mark the brand of victimization portrayed in the meeting with Hitler as having very particular repercussions, as representing the end of a journey.

F.'s and Edith's response to their encounter with Hitler offers us a parable of contemporary political complicity, implying that among the most sensitive, socially aware people there is a tendency to capitulate or even participate in the worst extremes of political violence. Within this tendency Cohen locates for us the perverse and irredeemable uses to which the images related to the Holocaust have been applied. His method of dealing with this material is unorthodox and provocative in the extreme, since he introduces the subject without providing any explicit polemical context by which the reader can gauge his attitude toward the Nazi genocide. He even goes so far as to present characters who have the sympathy of the reader, but who are also complicit in the dynamics of victimization enacted by the Nazis.

Cohen's approach, however, is not without its basis in well-documented phenomena. Historians see Hitler's totalitarian ideal as one that his followers took an active part in supporting and bringing into existence: "the 'heroic' Hitler image was 'as much an image created by the masses as it was imposed on them.' Propaganda was above all effective where it was building upon, not countering already existing values and mentalities" (Kershaw, *Hitler* 4). The fact that neither F. nor Edith is Jewish is worth noting, since it allows Cohen to investigate their yearnings for release through self-abuse without appearing to imply that Jews themselves identified with their torturers. Instead, the twosome can be seen as representative and prescient participants in the "Hitler Wave" that would erupt in the 1970s, "indicating a macabre fascination" with the Nazi leader (Kershaw, *Nazi* 62). While vacationing in a land notorious for honouring its hidden German war criminals, F. and Edith enact what a highly placed Nazi referred to at the Nuremberg trials as the "unlimited, almost religious veneration" that Hitler received from his associates (Kershaw, *Hitler* 263).

I would argue that Cohen's approach to these issues is scathingly honest in its effort to confront all the possible results of experimentation with excess, including a complicity with systems of dehumanization. Amid all the explosive and varied material included in *Beautiful Losers*, there is an ethical centre supported by Cohen's suggestion that the outcome of any eroticized interest in victimization and the abuse of power must inevitably bring about total demoralization and spiritual death.

The spectre of Hitler and, more generally, the ethos of Nazi and fascist culture have come to be aestheticized and eroticized in a wide variety of art, both highbrow and low. Writing in 1974, Susan Sontag described this trend as the rise of "Fascinating Fascism":

Art which evokes the themes of fascist aesthetic is popular now, and for most people it is probably no more than a variant of camp. Fascism may be merely fashionable, and perhaps fashion with its irrepressible promiscuity of taste will save us. But the judgments of taste themselves seem less innocent. Art that seemed eminently worth defending ten years ago, as a minority or adversary taste, no longer seems defensible today, because the ethical and cultural issues it raises have become serious, even dangerous. (97–8)

Beautiful Losers reflects this trend toward the lifting of a taboo against the use of Nazi imagery for entertainment and titillation. In the years following the novel's appearance, films by Fassbinder, Wertmuller, and Cavani, science fiction and spy novels, even camp role-playing within gay culture, all embraced the ethos of Nazism with a kind of nostalgia, fascination, and even a barely embarrassed reverence.[2]

This process of appropriation of images previously considered horrifying – too agonizing to contend with – as fair game for aesthetic or sexual practice is perversely exemplified in one review, quoted by Konrad Kellen, of Lina Wertmuller's 1976 film *Seven Beauties*. Judging the film to be an aesthetic success, the reviewer described how "he was always ashamed to have perceived a certain beauty in the way the corpses appeared in Auschwitz photos, but that since having seen *Seven Beauties* he no longer is ashamed to feel that way" (64). The acceptability of such attitudes toward aspects of the Holocaust marks an important shift from the approach taken by historians and artists in the immediate post-war years, as well as a re-emergence of attitudes that originally contributed to the Nazi rise to power. Again, the attraction of "emotions, images, and phantasms" raised by Nazism have gained an inexplicable hold over the popular imagination (Friedlander, *Reflections* 14). Writing in 1979, George Mosse warned of the danger of such developments: "Hitler as the pop hero and villain, Hitler as the central theme in an exciting drama – this is the result of the Hitler wave now upon us. Adolph Hitler has been taken over by the entertainment industry; books about his victims are in less demand. Indeed, the present Hitler revival comes uncomfortably close to presenting the Führer standing in splendid isolation without his subjects and without Auschwitz" ("Hitler" 21).

Beautiful Losers can be seen as anticipating the renewed attraction of Nazism and as offering a condemnation of the way that certain yearnings – psychological, sexual, or religious – can bring about extreme and inexcusable behaviour. The bedroom scene with Hitler offers the reader a grotesque parable of the movement from the abstract idea to the complicit act, from mere fascination to outright abuse, from *Mein Kampf* to Mauthausen. If F. has been in flight from the abyss of history in pursuit of ecstatic transcendence, then the diabolic scenario staged in his hotel room halts this flight, bringing into question all modes of thought on which such pursuits are founded.

Beautiful Losers is, in these terms, a *counter*-counter-culture work. Its popularity and notoriety have marked it, along with *Naked Lunch*, *On the Road*, and Allen Ginsberg's "Howl," as an exemplary case of 1960s art "with its scatological imagination, its mixture of pop culture, apocalyptic yearning, religiosity, and a kind of insane contemporary sociology" (Mandel, "Leonard" 209). Although Cohen's characters discover the expression of yearning through self-abuse and excess to offer certain satisfactions, the impulse is seen to be tainted by the disasters of modern history. The narrator, however unwittingly, mouths the kind of inanities that might have been uttered by a weary Nuremberger on his way to a Nazy Party rally: "I'm tired of facts," he says. "I'm tired of speculations, I want to be consumed by unreason. I want to be swept along" (49). Much of the excitement and fervour of Cohen's narrative comes from F.'s urging that he, the narrator, and Edith take an ennui-ridden plunge into ecstasy and instinct – what Dennis Lee calls a "dionysiac ontology" (77). There is no question that to some extent, Cohen himself is fascinated with this ontology and its excesses. It informed the Zeitgeist at the time of the novel's appearance, and Cohen himself perfected the role of spokesman, or at least that of fieldworker dedicated to the "insane" sociology of the time. But to the extent that *Beautiful Losers* can be read as indicative of his own state of mind, the bedroom scene with Hitler reveals his discomfort with this Zeitgeist, with his own pose as a hip, wiped-out sage dispensing pop philosophy from a bedroom at the Chelsea Hotel. In composing the scene set above an Argentinian beachfront, the novelist acknowledges that he has seen his own shadow – the part of his identity which he has not attended to or has cast out – and has recognized that it is "dominated by the presentiment and the memory of the Nazi horror" (Levinas, "Signature" 291).

3 Taking the Victims' Side: Mordecai Richler's Response to the Holocaust in *St. Urbain's Horseman*

The April 1993 opening of the Holocaust Memorial Museum in Washington, DC, prompted one commentator to address the role of "unembarrassed hatred" in the complex of feelings and judgments raised by the challenge of responding to the Holocaust. Leon Wieseltier argued that "hatred is not always the enemy of, or the obstacle to, understanding … certainly in the instance of radical evil, hatred may be evidence that a state of affairs has been properly understood" (24). Although Mordecai Richler does not write directly of hatred, his responses to the Nazis and their crimes acknowledge the inevitability of extreme reactions to extreme events. In an essay entitled "The Holocaust and After," he begins: "The Germans are still an abomination to me. I do not mourn for Cologne, albeit decimated for no useful military purpose. I rejoice in the crash of each German Starfighter. No public event in recent years has thrilled me more than the hunting down of Adolph Eichmann. I am not touched by the Berlin Wall"[1] (84). Quoting from Chaim Kaplan's Warsaw diary, Richler makes clear his agreement with the author's vehement, unforgiving abhorrence of German criminality: "Is there any revenge in the world for the spilling of innocent blood? I doubt it. The abominations committed before our eyes cry out from the earth. 'Avenge me!' But there is no jealous avenger. Why has a 'day of vengeance and retribution' not yet come for the murderers? Do not answer me with idle talk – I won't listen to you. Give me a logical reply!" (88)

Unembarrassed hatred of Nazi criminals and the imperative of vengeance are among the central themes of *St. Urbain's Horseman* (1971), published seven years after "The Holocaust and After." In the novel's opening scene Jake Hersh awakens from a dream in which Josef Mengele is tortured in the way that he and his Nazi compatriots tortured their victims in Auschwitz. Mengele's "gold fillings" are extracted "from the triangular cleft between his upper front teeth with pliers. Slowly, Jake thought ..." (2). And in a long list of lifelong fantasies yet to be accomplished, Jake affirms his longing for revenge: "I will be buried without ever having directed Olivier ... seen Jerusalem ... fought for a cause ... killed a Nazi" (49).

Richler's emphasis on unremitting anger at Nazi crimes and on the desire for revenge stands in contrast to a growing area of Holocaust research that focuses on the reception of the Nazi crimes as "trauma" and argues, in modified Freudian terms, for a "work of mourning" that will accomplish the "task of integrating damage, loss, disorientation, decenteredness into a transformed structure of identity, whether it be that of an individual, a culture, or an individual as a member of a cultural group" (Santner, *Stranded* xiii). This approach, undertaken by such scholars as Saul Friedlander, Dominick LaCapra, and Eric Santner, aims at resolving feelings of anger, shock, and defensiveness which burden the younger generation that was not directly touched by the Holocaust, whether they are the children of survivors or scholars at work in the field. By affirming the historian's task of questioning his or her own manner of confronting the Holocaust, such work supports a continuing commitment not only to telling history, but also to an examination of the "psychological dimension of the dilemmas facing postwar" reception of that history (Friedlander, *Probing* 11).

As Santner has described this approach, the reception of the Holocaust should be "theorized under the sign of massive trauma, meaning that these events must be confronted in their capacity to overwhelm the composition and coherence of individual and collective identities" ("History" 151). Such a perspective seems to suggest the view that the Holocaust is "unassimilated and unassimilable" (Friedlander, *Reflections* 11); in Shoshana Felman's words, it presents us with knowledge of events that leaves those who confront the Holocaust in survivors' or historians' accounts "at a loss, uprooted and disoriented, and profoundly shaken" in their "anchoring world views" (Felman and Laub xvi).

In his collection of essays, *Soundings in Critical Theory*, LaCapra suggests a rethinking of the relationship of certain Freudian concepts to the study of history, in order to enable, half a century after the event, a valid and creative response to the Holocaust. He does not advise the "application of psychoanalytic concepts to historical objects," in effect putting "individuals or groups from the past 'on the couch'" (32). He asks, rather, "how psychoanalysis can lead to a basic reconceptualization of historical self-understanding and practice" (32). LaCapra's key innovation is to apply the idea of transference, commonly used to describe the relationship between analyst and analysand, to an examination of the "relationship between any interpreter and an object of inquiry" (6). He writes of the "important but often unnoticed sense in which transference is at play in history, that is, in the very relation of the historian to the 'object' of study" (37). He argues that in a "transferential relation one tends to repeat in a displaced way the very processes that are active (at times uncritically) in one's object of inquiry" (6). Such unselfconscious repetition can lead a historian or author to *assume* rather than to *critique* certain roles that arise in accounts of the Holocaust, including that of perpetrator, victim, bystander, or resister. On a more subtle level, LaCapra says, the language and form of argumentation common to the Nazi era may even be replicated (or re-presented) rather than confronted and analysed.[2]

An appropriate approach to this difficult historical material, LaCapra argues, is the Freudian process of "working through" (*Durcharbeiten*), which implies an integration of loss and traumatic memories through a kind of "exchange" with the traumatic material, an effort to confront and enact a dialogue with it that will invoke a "cure," or at least a "counterweight" to mere "compulsive repetition," denial, emotional overreaction, or simplification (*Soundings* 41). He adds that "working through" the Holocaust "relies on a certain use of memory and judgment – a use that involves the critique of ideology, prominently including the critique of the scapegoat mechanism that had a historically specific and not simply arbitrary or abstract role in the Nazi treatment of the Jews" ("Representing" 24). Contrasted with "working through" is "acting out," a process in which the past is "compulsively repeated as if it were fully present, resistances are not confronted, and memory as well as judgment is disabled" (LaCapra, Rev. 178n).

It might be said that Jake Hersh, whom we first meet in the midst of a serious personal, but comically rendered crisis, is in need of a "counterweight" to his deeply held, but unresolved fascination with the Holocaust. Charged with the rape of his young German au pair and with "aiding and abetting sodomy," his family and his reputation in danger, he repeatedly flees from these problems by losing himself in his obsession with the Nazis' crimes and his frustration over being unable to avenge them (393). He is an inveterate newspaper clipper, and the walls of his "attic-study" are "plastered with photographs of wartime Nazi leaders and their survivors" (6). He fashions his "aerie" as a place where he can focus his energy – and his anger – on the escaped war criminal Josef Mengele. The wall clock is adjusted to "show the time in Paraguay – the *Doktor's* time"; it is to his aerie that Jake goes when he is awakened by his dreams of the *Doktor* (2–3). In a neurotically comic, but not entirely unserious way, the Holocaust seems to be "fully present" for Jake in his recurrent fantasies of the disasters that modern life might visit upon his family: "in Jake's Jewish nightmare, they come. Into his house. The extermination officers seeking out the Jew vermin. Ben is seized by the legs like a chicken and heaved out of the window, his brains spilling on the terrace. Molly, whose experience has led her to believe all adults gentle, is raised in the air not to be tossed and tickled, but to be flung against the brick fireplace. Sammy is dispatched with a pistol" (67).

St. Urbain's Horseman is shot through with references to Mengele, Auschwitz, Dachau, and anti-Semitism, yet this thematic material is treated on an emotional and personal level – often with more than a touch of black comedy – rather than from a philosophical or theological perspective. The hero in Jake's fantasies of revenge is his elusive cousin Joey, whom he remembers as a tough and glamorous figure from his boyhood on St Urbain Street in Montreal. To relieve his feelings of guilt for having settled for success as a film director in London, Jake worships the memory of Joey as an avenging "Horseman" who is relentless in his pursuit of Nazis such as Mengele. His cousin is his "moral editor," his "conscience, his mentor" (290, 433), who gives vicarious expression to his rebelliousness and dreams of unconventional, uncompromised individualism. Jake remembers Joey as a fighter with style, working out in his makeshift gym while glamorous women looked on (121). Like a figure out of Isaac Babel – a Jew on horseback – Joey rode at "the Bagg Street stables" while Jake sat on his mother's front step (122). St Urbain Street legend has it that Joey played semi-pro baseball and piloted a plane (123). He was supposedly sighted in action in Spain in 1938 and in Israel a decade later, and now Jake imagines him in Paraguay hunting down Josef Mengele. Joey is a convenient figure on whom Jake can project his "causes," especially his desire for action, which has been frustrated by his comfortable life as a "husband, father, house owner, investor, sybarite, and film fantasy-spinner" (289).

As he becomes ever more dejected about the significance of his own accomplishments, Jake fantasizes increasingly about the exploits of his cousin: "The less satisfaction his work gave him, even as he drifted on the crest of the television plateau, having done everything he could there and beginning to repeat himself, the more he began to talk about his cousin Joey, speculating about his where-abouts, wondering what he was really like, oddly convinced that somehow Joey had answers for him" (214). In Joey, Jake fashions the image of a paragon of daring and effective action. And by imagining his cousin on the trail of Mengele, Jake creates a self-validating link between his own comfortable life and the suffering of the Holocaust.

His awareness of how remote his own experience in the war years was from that of the Jews of Europe contributes to his sense of inadequacy and self-loathing. He worries that he has come to resemble the hard-working, prudent Jews of Montreal that he detested as a youth:

As Franco strutted into Madrid, a conqueror, Jake and his friends sat on the St. Urbain Street stoop and mourned the benching of Lou Gehrig, their first hint of mortality. The invasion of Poland was photographs they pasted into the opening pages of World War II scrapbooks, coming in a season they cherished for *The Wizard of Oz*. Unlike their elder brothers, they could only conjecture about how they would have reacted in battle. They collected aluminum pots for Spitfires and waited impatiently for the war's end so that Billy Conn could get his second chance. The holocaust was when their parents prospered on the black market and they first learned the pleasures of masturbation. If, as secure and snotty ten-year-olds, they mocked those cousins and uncles who were too prudent to enlist, then it was an appren-ticeship appropriate to encroaching middle age, when they were to exhort younger men to burn their draft cards. From pint-size needlers, callow fans in the wartime bleachers, they had matured to moral coaches, the instigators of petitions, without ever having been tried on the field themselves. The times had not used but compromised them. Too young to have marched into gunfire in Europe, they were also too old and embarrassed, too fat, to wear the flag as underwear. (80–1)

Through Joey, Jake identifies with the activists of history, the men who battled against evil. Joey's rumoured presence in the Spanish Civil War, in the Israeli War of Independence, and now, in Jake's fantasies, in Paraguay give Jake a sense of being engaged himself.

The basis for his fantasies about Joey lies in his own experience of anti-Semitism when he was a boy in wartime Montreal. He recalls the altercations between Québécois and Jew as scenes of instruction, as primal battles that became integral to the way in which he views his place in the world. He remembers the bullying of Jews by Québécois nationalists and bigots, and his Uncle Abe's astonishment at seeing "À bas les Juifs" painted along the highway. In town "the windows in Jewish shops were being broken and swastikas … painted on the pavement outside the shul on Fairmount Street." Yet despite such challenges and attacks, and despite the vandalism by "roaming gangs of truculent French Canadians," Jewish community leaders – Uncle Abe among them – publicly reaffirmed their commitment to the anti-Semitic Union Nationale government. Jake recalls with disgust how proud these men were to be photographed with a government minister, "shaking hands and smiling benignly on the steps outside the Château Frontenac in Quebec City" (124–5).

In St. Urbain's Horseman the familiar streets off the Main are a zone of contention, primarily between Jewish heroism and Jewish submission. Only Joey, according to Jake, embraced the former course of action. His return to St Urbain Street after years of mysterious absence is immediately seen as a threat to community relations when he refuses to accept anti-Jewish slurs passively. He belittles his elders' reluctance to fight back, mocking their caution, and he leads a band of Jewish toughs in a retributive raid on the Palais d'Or (126). Joey's example inspires young Jake to see himself as a rebel, though he acts out this rebelliousness against the easy targets of Canadian stodginess and provinciality in the post-war years and the Jewish bourgeoisie of Montreal.

Richler does not resort in the novel to the invidious stereotype of the Nazis' victims going quietly "as sheep to the slaughter," but the valorization of action and resistance over compromise and passivity comes close to invoking this simplistic interpretation of the Holocaust. The inability of the Jews to defend themselves against Nazi violence, alongside the politic unwillingness of the Jews of Montreal to meet violence with violence, inform Jake's impassioned interest in Joey, Mengele, and St Urbain Street. It is to challenge and repudiate the role of the Jew as victim that Jake creates the image of Joey as an avenging Horseman "cantering on a magnificent Pleven stallion. Galloping, thundering" to find Mengele, the "angel of death" of Auschwitz, to whom he would mete out just retribution (244).

Jake imagines Joey's interests to be firmly fixed on the perpetrators and on avenging Nazi crimes, rather than on the victims and their suffering. Jake's interest is not so monomaniacal; he ruminates over the testimony of Auschwitz guards as they describe the torments and degradations of the camp (67), and broods over one of the most famous images of the Holocaust: "the familiar photograph of a bewildered little Jewish boy, wearing a cap, a torn pullover, and shorts, his eyes aching with fear as he raises his arms over his head. There are other Jews huddled together on this narrow street in Warsaw. Wearing caps, supporting bundles. All of them, with arms raised" (66).

Jake's obsessions, continuing anger, and anxiety are intensified by the reports that he reads of the Frankfurt trial of Auschwitz guards. Beginning in December 1963 and continuing into 1965, it was "the longest jury trial in German legal history" (Naumann vii). Its aim was to bring to justice representatives of the low- and middle-ranking Nazis who beat, tortured, and murdered prisoners on their own initiative. Verbatim testimony from this trial haunts Jake as he searches Frankfurt's *jazzkellers* for Joey, whom he believes might be in Germany to watch the proceedings. Richler includes from this testimony a well-known and horrifyingly matter-of-fact description of the dead after a gas chamber is opened:

The bodies are not lying scattered here and there throughout the room, but piled in a mass to the ceiling. This is explained by the fact that the gas first inundates the lower layers of air and rises but slowly to the ceiling. That forces them to trample and clamber over one another. At the bottom of the pile are the babies, children, women and aged; at the top, the strongest. Their bodies which bear numerous scratches occasioned by the struggle which set them against one another, are often intertwined. The noses and mouths are bleeding, the faces bloated and blue. (245)

Richler also quotes from testimony given by an Auschwitz survivor, Arie Fuks, of Mengele's activities:

"Were there also other methods of killing children?"
" ... I saw them take a child from its mother, carry it over to Crematory IV, which had two big pits, and throw the child into the seething human fat ..."

"Mengele cannot have been there all the time."
"In my opinion, always. Night and day." (254; Naumann 272)

Richler does not contextualize or philosophize about the Frankfurt trial or the issues that it raises, and his protagonist shows no interest in such rumination. Richler's method of simply including the material in his fiction is in stark contrast with that of William Styron, who quotes from and summarizes the theories of George Steiner, Hannah Arendt, and others in *Sophie's Choice*. For Jake, the crimes described at the Frankfurt trial remain an enraging enigma, a source of anger and disgust rather than a starting point for philosophy.

The Frankfurt trial provided ample evidence that eighteen years after the Nazi defeat the murderers were not ashamed before the victims who remained to accuse them. In an introduction to the published testimony of the trial, Arendt comments on "the behaviour of the defendants – in their laughing, smiling, smirking impertinence toward prosecution and witness, their lack of respect for the court" (xii). The trial also made clear the difficulty of judging the crimes committed in the death camps in a traditional judicial environment. Naumann notes that although twenty-three defendants were charged and found guilty of crimes including "accessory" to murder, murder, and "having played a role in the implementation of the National Socialist extermination program," the appeal process rendered all the verdicts legally inoperative (419–26). Arendt is unsure, in her introductory remarks, whether these men were in prison or if they had "gone home" while their cases were under appeal (xvii). The inappropriateness of the trial's outcome and the inadequacy of judicial proceedings in dealing with Nazi crimes lead

Jake to focus on Josef Mengele, the embodiment of Nazi evil, and he is thrilled when he discovers what he takes to be evidence that Joey was also obsessed with Mengele. When Jake visits one of his cousin's abandoned wives in Israel, he is shown what Joey left behind when he disappeared:

yellowing newspaper and magazine photographs. Rosy-cheeked *gemütlich* Frau Goering going about her shopping on the Theatinerstrasse. The austere Von Papen family, the eldest boy named Adolph, posing on a leather chesterfield. "Sepp" Dietrich looking severe. There were also well-worn pages from a journal, describing the activities of Josef Mengele, philosophy student and chief doctor at Auschwitz, who lived quietly in Munich until 1951, when he fled over the Reschenpass-Merano route to Italy, with the help of ODESSA, and from there to Spain, then Buenos Aires, and when the Perón regime collapsed in 1955, to Paraguay. (242)

Jake's respect for the Horseman is motivated by his own feelings of irrelevancy in the face of the Nazis' crimes. Intertwined with his obsessive fear of violent death and his uneasiness about his affluent and happy life is a deeply felt and complicated compulsion to *do something* about the Holocaust. But apart from the quoted testimony at the Frankfurt trial, the Holocaust is never anything other than a phantasm haunting his daily life. Clinging to the memory of a youthful Joey standing up to anti-Semitic harassment, Jake creates a counter-phantasm, a hero who abhorred passivity and exhorted his elders, "mocking them, asking them what they intended to do about such insults" (125). Joey's militancy becomes a touchstone for Jake, and his cousin's words return at the novel's conclusion. Though Joey is reported dead "in an air crash, between the Mato Grosso and the Brazilian Highlands, not far from the Paraná River" (433), Jake hears his voice demanding, *"What are you going to do about it"* (433). Jake's response to this query is to cross out the notation that he has made in the Horseman's journal regarding his death, "July 20, 1967, in an air crash," in favour of the note "presumed dead" (433, 436). Ironically, rather than take on his cousin's supposed heroic wanderings himself, Jake simply extends his faith in the Horseman, continuing to fantasize that his hero is unkillable, a kind of avenging angel.

Eschewing the type of ethical, philosophical, or religious responses to the Holocaust offered in other Canadian and American novels, Richler does not present the survivor figure as an exemplar of human dignity whose ability to renew his or her life stands in opposition to atrocity. In the work of A.M. Klein, Philip Roth, and Saul Bellow the survivor is depicted as an ideal figure from whom others can learn how to respond to the claims of Jewish identity and history in the wake of the Holocaust. By contrast, Richler, with a certain irony, chooses a different type of survivor as a model for his protagonist, a rough vagabond and rebel who is described by Jake's Uncle Abe as "a blackmailer … a gambler and a bigamist and a liar. You and I are discussing a gigolo. A man who moves from country to country under assumed names, certainly with good reason" (385).

Rather than allowing him to come to terms with the Holocaust and Jewish life after the war, Jake's obsession with the Horseman seems only to provide encouragement for his fantasies of threat and revenge, as well as fuel for his urge to see himself as a potential victim. His defensiveness and his fantasy-spinning bear strong similarities to the process that Santner calls "narrative fetishism," which he sees as related to the "work of mourning." Both are "strategies whereby groups and individuals reconstruct their vitality and identity in the wake of trauma. The crucial difference between the two modes of repair has to do with the willingness or capacity to include the traumatic event in one's efforts to reformulate and reconstitute identity" ("History" 152).

Narrative fetishism, however, according to Santner, inhibits this capacity through "the construction and deployment of a narrative consciously or unconsciously designed to expunge the traces of the trauma or loss that called that narrative into being in the first place" ("History" 144). Like acting out, it disables memory and judgment and inhibits the desirable aim of reconstituting identity: "it is a strategy of undoing, in fantasy, the need for mourning by simulating a condition of intactness" (144). Jake's belief in Joey as a kind of latter-day golem, a "Jewish Batman," follows this model (252). Rather than helping him to accommodate or analyse the fear and loss that he feels – integrating those feelings into a new identity – Jake's imagined bond with his cousin focuses his desire on the implausible prospect of revenge, on *doing something*. It might be argued that he strives to "expunge the traces of trauma" he feels over his inability to reverse or avenge the Holocaust by repeatedly fantasizing that Joey will do something, that the Horseman will make things fit again.

Through most of the novel, Jake's pained fascination with the Holocaust provides him with no creative suggestion of how to live in post-war culture; he seems unable to enter into any dialogue with the past that will generate "viable institutions of both discourse and social life that effectively resist the recurrence of anything comparable to the Nazi regime" (LaCapra, "Representing" 126). He is stricken by fear, self-doubt, and a feeling of incompatibility with a world that he holds in contempt, and he can see no alternative to the culture in which he lives and which he sees as complicit as well as corrupted. It seems almost inevitable that this impasse will lead him toward the kind of self-destructive friendship he nurtures with Harry Stein, who represents the ugly face of uncompromising Jewish self-defiance.

It is Jake's reliance on the fantasy figure of Joey as icon and protector that inhibits him from investigating his own fears. But through his entanglement with Harry Stein, he distances himself from these fantasies, and in doing so he makes a more critical "use of memory and judgement." In more ways than one Harry is Jake's nemesis. It is he who makes Jake appear to have taken advantage of the au pair girl; his access to Jake's creatively managed tax returns brings about an audit by British Internal Revenue (336). Harry's malice, however, is motivated by more than generalized resentment of the downtrodden: he plays on Jake's loyal attachment to the image of his cousin to demand restitution for money that Joey apparently stole from the woman who is now Harry's girlfriend. He becomes a focus for Jake's guilt about his neglected idealism – his leftish respect for the underdog, the victimized, the losers of the world:

Bony little Harry, a veritable bantam, wore a pullover under his jacket and a CND badge on his lapel. The badge was redundant, for his manner bespoke sufficiently of inherited discontent exacerbated by experience. Black, wintry experience. Jake immediately recognized in him the deprived man seething at the end of the bus queue in the driving rain. As he hurtled past in a taxi. It was Harry who called on his way home for a gallon of Esso Pink and lit the Aladdin before setting out the Birdseye frozen potato chips and Walls sausages for his solitary supper. While Jake upbraided the butcher at Harrod's, demanding and getting a thicker, better-hung slice of Scotch rump. Harry who joined the Christmas club in July and endured talley-men and was not chagrined by the cutback in bank overdrafts. Or the waiting list for Jaguars. Or the ski conditions at Klosters. Or the punitive capital gains tax. Harry whom the world insulted. (57)

Harry is also one of those whom history has touched directly. The Second World War was not a time of adolescent sexual high jinks and ballpark pranks for him, but the Blitz, harassment, and under-nourishment.

When their trial concludes, Jake is treated kindly by the court, while Harry, lacking Jake's connections and polish, bears its harshest punishment. He is sentenced to five years in prison and dismissed as a human being: "You are a humbug, Stein, and a troublemaker of the most reprehensible sort. In my opinion, what we need is an island, somewhere where people like you could be sent" (420). Jake is let off with a lecture, having been described by the prosecutor in a way that undermines his tendency to view himself with self-pity: "well-educated, successful, talented, married, with three children. He lives in style, mingling with cinema stars in Mayfair's most fash-ionable restaurants. *Look at it this way. He is so successful in his chosen field that he earns rather more annually than the prime minister of this country*" (416; Richler's italics). By setting Jake's self-perceived victim status in the context of the trial at the Old Bailey, Richler mocks, with affection, his fears and implies that Jake is aware of his tendency to overdramatize his situation. He intimates that Jake's well-developed sense of threat has more to do with his personal feelings of inadequacy – with his sense of his own insignificant role in history – than with his actual standing in society.

In the novel's climactic scene, where Jake learns of Joey's death, Richler intimates that he has managed to overcome his feelings of loss and his unworked-through relationship with history's trauma. Jake weeps at the end of *St. Urbain's Horseman*, but not so much for Joey and the Holocaust's victims as for all the unfinished business in his own life, the compromises, disappointments, and betrayals that he has never come to terms with.

He wept … The tears he couldn't coax out of himself at his father's graveside or summon up for Mr. Justice Beal's verdict on Harry or his mother's departure flowed freely now. Torn from his soul, the tears welled in his throat and ran down his cheeks. He whimpered, he moaned. He sank, trembling, to the sofa. He wept for his father, his penis curling out of his underwear like a spent worm. His penis, my maker. Rotting in an oversize pinewood casket. He wept for his mother, who deserved a more loving son. He wept for Harry, fulminating in his cell and assuredly planning vengeance. (433)

Here Richler seems to suggest that the Holocaust is not, in any essential way, Jake's trauma in the form of unmourned or unresolved history. It is instead one of the realms of fantasy within which Jake imagines acts of idealistic struggle designed to overcome his feelings of inadequacy and disaffection from mainstream society. The Holocaust might be said to be "good material" for him, allowing him an opportunity to express a sensitivity to the suffering of the people from whom he has distanced himself, as well as concern for the profound issues of good and evil that it represents. Through its intricate plot and black humour, *St. Urbain's Horseman* dramatizes the process, described by Santner, by which we accommodate history: "the stories one tells about the past (and, more specifically, about how one came to be who one is or thinks one is) are at some level determined by the present social, psychological, and political needs of the teller" ("History" 143).

Richler seems to be aware of these determinants in the way that he presents and then contextualizes Jake's Holocaust fantasies. Jake is too much inclined to apply his skills as a "fantasy-spinner" to the events of the war (289). It is this tendency in the work of Elie Wiesel that Richler criticizes in "The Holocaust and After." Characterizing *Night* as the "one book about the holocaust that should be obligatory reading," he nevertheless says about Wiesel's other writings that when he "strays from his direct experience of the *shtetl*, the death camps and after, when he attempts to spin tales, an indulgence readily permitted to the rest of us, I find myself impatient. Unjustifiably, perhaps, but impatient just the same" (95). In *St. Urbain's Horseman*, despite his affection for Jake, Richler ultimately wants us to feel an impatience with him and relief when, at the novel's conclusion, he appears to consider laying aside his fantasy of the Horseman.

Here it is worth considering the relationship between Richler himself and his protagonist. The wealth of similarity between the personal résumés of the actual writer and the fictional "fantasy-spinner" is enough to lend *St. Urbain's Horseman* the character of a veiled intellectual autobiography. Yet in an essay entitled "Why I Write," Richler makes it clear that he does not share Jake's troubling and compulsive relationship with the Holocaust. Describing the five years that he spent working on the novel, he does not mention any unusual unease posed by the challenge of dealing with the gas chambers, transit trains, and Mengele's awful experiments; he cites instead the dreariness of authorial isolation, "fatigue and distractions" (20). He does not dismiss, however, the danger and likelihood of what LaCapra calls "acting out," the tendency to respond to the past through emotional overreaction or simplification. In "The Holocaust and After," Richler acknowledges a tendency, in the press, in the Jewish community, and in bad art, to make use of the Holocaust's impact for frivolous and self-serving purposes: "In 1960, in Montreal, I heard a fatuous suburban rabbi invoke the six million in a plea for funds to build a synagogue banquet hall. In Leeds, several years later ... I came across an editorial against inter-marriage, in the Jewish Gazette, which concluded, 'Hitler did his evil best to wipe out the Jewish people. It seems that if we don't look out we will finish the job for him,' as if marriage to a Yorkshire shiksa was comparable to a trip to the gas ovens" (93).

Jake, we must assume, is a type that Richler recognized among compatriots and peers, a man of his time who was worth examining. Indeed, Richler's portrait of Jake Hersh's inner life bears an uncanny resemblance to the portrait that Alain Finkielkraut draws of a whole generation of French men and women who came of age, like Jake, in the early sixties. Paradigmatic among these, Finkielkraut suggests, was the writer and leftist agitator Pierre Goldman, who described himself in terms almost identical to those that Jake uses:

A tribunal sat inside me, governed by a pitiless law, and before that tribunal I stood condemned only when confronted by my dreams, my ideals. Justice could not punish me, because, in my crimes, I had *already* punished myself. These crimes were not the offense of having stolen money by armed robbery. Rather, they were acts by which I had punished myself for not having been my father, a partisan, for not having been Marcel Rayman, for not having fought beside Che, beside Marighella, for not having tracked down Borman in order to kill him. (qtd. in Finkielkraut 27)

Goldman was afraid, Finkielkraut argues, of "failing to resemble the heroes of the concentration camps who haunted his memory" (26), of falling into the role of Jewish submission and individual defeat that Jake fears, rather than pledging himself to public commitment and heroism.

St. Urbain's Horseman is a trial-haunted book. Jake hovers about the site of the Frankfurt trial of Auschwitz guards hoping to contact the Horseman.[3] The Eichmann trial was still being hotly debated – Eichmann was hanged in 1962 – as Richler began work on his novel three years later. And Jake himself is subjected to his own trial, both in a court of law and before his family and friends. The Frankfurt trial ended inconclusively, with the convictions set aside on a legal technicality. There were many who felt that the hanging of Eichmann "constituted an inappropriate ending," an act of vengeance that would not bring about the "different education of men and nations, a new human awareness" (Scholem 299). Gershom Scholem's dissatisfaction with the manner in which Israel dealt with Eichmann reminds us of LaCapra's warning that confrontation with a traumatic past must be based on "a certain use of memory and judgement," a confrontation with it that will integrate feelings of damage and loss into "a transformed structure of identity" (Santner, *Stranded* xiii).

It is exactly this kind of transformation that Jake undergoes in the aftermath of his own trial, as it, along with the news of the Horseman's death, triggers a renewed investigation of his own experience of loss. This sense of loss is not tied to his fantasies of Joey's heroism, nor is it informed by the compulsive fear that has led him to draw comparisons between himself and the victims of the Holocaust. Jake's problems are many, but the Holocaust is not essentially one of them. He knows a great deal about it, and when he is not applying this knowledge to his personal fantasies, it leads him to a straightforward appreciation of the "plain meaning of the story," as well as to an attendant attitude of "condemnation accompanied by an intensity of feeling" (Wieseltier 24).

PART TWO

Strange Presences

Forethought:
Facing Up to the Past

"Who expresses himself according to his heart about men?" asks
the French philosopher Emmanuel Levinas. "Who shows them his
face?" These questions, even after they have been translated from
Levinas's more evocative French, have the uncanny power momen-
tarily to stop the heart. *What does the man mean?* the reader might
well wonder. Could he be addressing such queries to *me*? But then,
if we allow Levinas's questions to resonate, to unsettle our everyday
selves, we may recognize that his provocations provide an excellent
framework for our consideration of contemporary Jewish writing,
where the face, as a guiding symbol for commitment to others,
returns again and again. Following Levinas further, we find in his
description of the face "a demand ... The face is a hand in search
of recompense, an open hand. That is it needs something. It is going
to ask you for something ... It is the frailty of the one who needs
you, who is counting on you" ("Paradox" 169–71). A demand. An
open hand. A question. The prospect of a contract to be honoured.
These are among the effects brought about by the appearance of a
trio of faces conjured in the work of Philip Roth and Chava Rosenfarb – the faces of dead writers with features as familiar as those in
a family portrait.

4 Strange Presences on the Family Tree: The Unacknowledged Literary Father in Philip Roth's *The Prague Orgy*

Philip Roth's fascination with Franz Kafka is well known, and throughout Roth's career the diffident son of an overbearing Prague businessman has served as his paradigm for the contradictions of filial love and resentment. This makes it all the more noteworthy that in *The Prague Orgy*, the novella that Roth appended as an epilogue to his Zuckerman Trilogy, he makes use of the life and work of a lesser-known Jewish Polish writer in his depiction of Nathan Zuckerman's struggles with cultural inheritance and literary influence in Prague. In a subtly worked scenario that turns the reader into a kind of literary sleuth, Roth adds Bruno Schulz to his carnival of literary and not-so-literary father figures. Schulz is never mentioned by name – the biographical details of his life and work are manipulated and purposely disguised, turned into what Roth has called "useful fiction" (*Reading* 106) – but through plot turns and oblique references he becomes a ghostly presence in the narrative of *The Prague Orgy*.[1]

After his death at the hand of a Gestapo officer in 1942, Bruno Schulz's reputation as a writer of eccentric, magical fictions was buried, like much of the fragile culture of middle and eastern Europe, beneath the rubble of a ghetto. His final manuscript, *The Messiah*, as well as much of his correspondence, was lost, and his two published collections of fiction, entitled *Cinnamon Shops* and *Sanatorium under the Sign of the Hourglass*, remained virtually unknown in the West until Philip Roth included them in his Writers from the Other Europe series. Published by Penguin alongside Milan Kundera, Danilo Kis, and Tadeusz Borowski, Schulz gained an international readership. Cynthia Ozick contributed to North American readers' familiarity with him by placing him at the centre of her novel *The Messiah of Stockholm* (1987), which Ozick dedicated to Roth, perhaps in gratitude for his efforts at gaining Schulz a readership in America. And Isaac Bashevis Singer spoke warmly of his *lantsman*, telling Roth that he favoured Schulz's writing above Kafka's (Roth, "Roth and Singer" 5).

As an editor for Penguin, Roth was responsible for the recovery of a valuable literary patrimony, but in his fictional mining of Schulz's life and work, he betrays a rather complicated and ambiguous attitude toward this resurrected literary hero. *The Prague Orgy* is introduced as an extract "from Zuckerman's notebooks," beginning with an entry dated 11 January 1976 (423). Roth began working with Penguin on the Writers from the Other Europe series in 1974, and Schulz's *Cinnamon Shops* appeared under the title *The Street of Crocodiles* three years later[2] (Rodgers 22, 374). During the period when he was involved with Penguin on *Cinnamon Shops*, the details of Schulz's life and work made such a strong impact on Roth that they reappeared as thematic concerns in his fiction. Interestingly enough, Schulz does not appear in Roth's novella as the recipient of a literary heir's unquestioning worship. Rather, he is portrayed in *The Prague Orgy* as another of the author's elusive fathers, as a link with a lost heritage, but also as a questionable figure of authority, one who is at once inspiring and loved, but forever out of reach.

Nathan Zuckerman's search for an appropriate literary father figure begins in *The Ghost Writer*, the first volume of the Zuckerman Trilogy. The "amiable" relationship that Nathan enjoys with his own father has been upset by his first published work, and his arrival on the doorstep of "the most famous literary ascetic in America" is guided by the desire to be accepted as E.I. Lonoff's "spiritual son" (7). In *The Prague Orgy* an admirer brings a plan for the recovery of a literary patrimony to the door of Nathan Zuckerman's Manhattan apartment. Now a mature and successful writer himself, Zuckerman attracts his own acolytes, and it is an exiled and bitter Czech named Zdenek Sisovsky who comes begging for help in an effort to regain his patrimony. Sisovsky asks Zuckerman to help him recover his father's unpublished stories, an "elliptical, humble, self-conscious" body of work written in Yiddish in the style of Flaubert (434–5). This Flaubertian œuvre is under the protection of Sisovsky's ex-wife in Prague, who, he believes, will surrender the manuscript to a "famous, attractive, American genius who does not practice the American innocence to a shameless degree" (435).

Throughout Roth's Zuckerman books, strangers, driven by the belief that they "understand" the famous writer, accost him and make demands. In *Zuckerman Unbound*, Alvin Pepler demands the return of his life, a commodity that he believes Zuckerman stole from him by using it for his notorious best-seller (202). In *The Counterlife*, another manic, fawning ex-Newarker, Jimmy Lustig, demands Zuckerman's fatherly approval and his aid in a hijacking attempt (167). For characters such as Alvin Pepler, West Orange's Jimmy Lustig, and Zdenek Sisovsky, it is Zuckerman's fame, his mythic trouble-making, establishment-baiting persona, that marks him as a hero. Nathan wonders if Sisovsky has even read his novels, as he muses on how the "ruined exile will not be deflected from commiserating with the American success" (ZB 424). But he undertakes Sisovsky's odyssey of retrieval all the same.

The author of the manuscript that Zuckerman sets out to recover in Prague is a Czech Yiddishist who fathered two children by a Czech wife and was murdered by the Gestapo in 1941 (432–3). Bruno Schulz was an assimilated Jew who wrote in Polish; in fact, he had little to do with the large Polish Yiddish literary community. He had no wife or children, and he was killed in November 1942 (Ficowski, *Letters* 248). But here the discrepancies between the fictional murdered Jew, Sisovsky, and the more famous literary victim of the Gestapo cease. The story that Sisovsky tells of his father's death is worthy of close attention:

In our town there was a Gestapo officer who loved to play chess. After the occupation began, he found out that my father was the chess master of the region, and so he had him to his house every night. My father was horribly shy of people, even of his students. But because he believed that my mother and my brother would be protected if he was courteous with the officer, he went whenever he was called. And they *were* protected. All the Jews in town were huddled into the Jewish quarter. For the others things got a little worse every day, but not for my family. For more than a year nobody bothered them. My father could no longer teach at the high school, but he was now allowed to go around as a private tutor to earn some money. At night, after our dinner, he would leave the Jewish quarter and go to play chess with the Gestapo officer. Well, stationed in town was another Gestapo officer. He had a Jewish dentist whom *he* was protecting … One Sunday, a Sunday probably much like today, the two Gestapo officers went out drinking together and they got drunk … They had an argument. They were good friends, so it must have been a terrible argument, because the one who played chess with my father was so angry that he walked over to the dentist's house and got the dentist out of bed and shot him. This enraged the other Nazi so much that the next morning he came to our house and he shot my father. (432–3)

The details of Sisovsky's narrative bear a strong similarity to the circumstances under which Bruno Schulz spent his last months. In his case, however, it was not chess, but the writer's dreamlike drawings, tinged with sadomasochism, that charmed the local Gestapo officer. With a special pass, Schulz was able to venture into the "Aryan" quarter of his town, a small community called Drogobych in southeastern Poland. On one such visit he was recognized by an SS officer who was a rival of his protector and was shot (Wieniewska 9–10). The similarities between the elder Sisovsky and Schulz do not stop at this grisly narrative. The former is said to have been a high school mathematics teacher in a provincial town, while Schulz taught art at a secondary school for boys in Drogobych (ZB 432). Zdenek's description of his father as being "horribly shy of people" parallels Jerzy Ficowski's appraisal of Schulz as a recluse who "maintain[ed] contact with those near to him through letters. In this way he alleviated his isolation without having it disturbed by any outside presence" (Ficowski, Intro. 14) The "introverted" father whom Zdenek describes writing "for himself" (ZB 432) could well have characterized the "overriding motif" of his personal fate as a "profound loneliness, isolation from the stuff of daily life" (Ficowski, *Letters* 114). Bruno Schulz included this self-appraisal in an essay written for Stanislaw Witkiewicz, Poland's leading cultural figure before the war, who tried unsuccessfully to lure his solitary friend away from his sleepy provincial home.

After the publication of *The Street of Crocodiles*, Roth published several accounts of his discovery and appreciation of Schulz's work, in which the issue of the writer's precarious position as a Jew writing in Polish between the wars comes up repeatedly (Roth, "Roth and Singer" 5). In an interview with Roth, I.B. Singer suggests that Schulz developed his parodic style "because he was not really at home, neither at home among the Poles nor among the Jews" (16). Such writers as Schulz, according to Singer, were thought of by the Polish literati as "intruders" (14). In the same interview, Singer and Roth discuss whether Schulz or Kafka suffered from a deeper sense of homelessness and alienation. Roth repeats Kafka's well-known remark on his communal affiliations: "What have I in common with the Jews? I have hardly anything in common with myself and should stand very quietly in the corner, content that I can breathe" (20). To this Singer adds his impression of Schulz's inability to find a place for himself in *any* literary community: "in Warsaw he felt he ought to get back to Drogobych because in Warsaw everybody said, 'Who is Schulz?' Writers are not really ready to see a young man from the provinces and immediately to say, 'You are our brother, you are our teacher' ... Also, he was a Jew ... When there came another Jew who writes Polish, they felt not really comfortable about it" (20).

This discussion is fictionalized in *The Prague Orgy*, with the elder Sisovsky taking Schulz's place in the comparison with Kafka. Zdenek explains that his father "never thought he was a real Czech," and that because of this his stories dwell upon a "homelessness beyond homelessness. One story is called 'Mother Tongue.' Three pages only, about a little Jewish boy who speaks bookish German, Czech without the native flavor, and the Yiddish of people simpler than himself. Kafka's homelessness, if I may say so, was nothing beside my father's. Kafka had at least the nineteenth century in his blood – all those Prague Jews did. Kafka belonged to literature, if nothing else. My father belonged to nothing" (434). Zdenek's apologetic tone, in deference to the great Kafka, echoes Singer's hesitation to set Schulz above Prague's most famous literary son. But Zdenek's complimentary attitude toward his father quickly gives way to criticism, as the younger Sisovsky belittles his father's tendency toward self-mortification and inner torment. He ends his account of his father with a rhetorical flourish that Zuckerman himself might choose as a manifesto for his own most agonized afternoons: "What is this man so lonely for? Why is he so sad and withdrawn? He should join the revolution – then he would not sit with his head in his hands, wondering where he belongs" (434).

Of course, Zdenek the exile does not "belong" in New York. And his "boring European" story relates not only to the Czech, Sisovsky, a Yiddishist among "people simpler than himself"; it also resurrects the ghost of Bruno Schulz, a Jew not at home among his own people nor among the Poles from whose language he distilled his unique mythopoeia (432–4). To this list of displaced writers we can add our "famous, attractive, American genius" (435) Nathan Zuckerman, whose predicament has been characterized by one critic as the experience of "disinheritance from those he must write about" combined with a "responsibility to their history" (H. Lee 70). Zuckerman, like Zdenek, Sisovsky senior, and Bruno Schulz, is constantly agonizing over what to be and with whom, and how to overcome the urge to "sit with his head in his hands, wondering where he belongs."

These crises of identity ultimately all lead back to fathers – to the appraisal by sons of their inheritance, of their mother tongue, of their sense of place in the society into which they are born. Both Schulz and the elder Sisovsky were the sons of village shopkeepers. Their literary aspirations set them apart from their fathers' world, and they are, in different degrees, both sons, not of their fathers' Jewish workaday world, but of a European secularism born of the Enlightenment. Sisovsky read "Lessing, Herder, Goethe, and Schiller" (434). In his letters, Schulz makes a plea to a friend in Warsaw for a copy of Husserl (151); to him Rilke is "godlike" (37), and Goethe leaves him "shaken to the bottom of [his] soul" (111). Yet Schulz's first inclination was to call *Cinnamon Shops* "Reminiscences of Father," and Father appears throughout the volume as one of Schulz's most startling mythical beings. This pattern of retreat from and fascination with the world of one's father is duplicated in I.B. Singer's autobiography, *In My Father's Court*. Singer presents his father as a man whose attachment to things spiritual was a source of succour, but whose tendency to "lash out with great vehemence against worldly pleasures" was endlessly frustrating for his open-eyed and curious son (23).

All of this leads us back to the elder Zuckerman, who is in some ways the American version of a European village shopkeeper. He is "superconventional" (*Counterlife* 112), a chiropodist with a keen sense of communal values, and he is, for Nathan, a source of both pride and shame. At the beginning of the Zuckerman Trilogy he is an obstruction, the source of a stultifying form of conventional moral reprobation. He insists that his son's literary aspirations be focused on a kind of cultural-historical propaganda "about the scientists and teachers and lawyers [American Jews] become and the things such people accomplish for others ... about the immigrants ... who worked and saved and sacrificed to get a decent footing in America" (ZB 57). But elsewhere in the trilogy the elder Zuckerman attains nothing less than mythical status. In *The Anatomy Lesson*, Nathan pays homage to "old-fashioned fathers," portraying the balance between authority and gentleness that men such as Victor Zuckerman struck:

Who that follows after us will understand how midway through the twentieth century, in this huge, lax, disjointed democracy, a father – and not even a father of learning or eminence or demonstrable power – could still assume the stature of a father in a Kafka story? No, the good old days are just about over, when half the time, without even knowing it, a father could sentence a son to punishment for his crimes and the love and hatred of authority could be such a painful, tangled mess. (413)

Roth uses Kafka's agonized relationship with his father as an example against which to examine his own struggle with patriarchal expectations in an essay entitled "'I Always Wanted You to Admire My Fasting'; or, Looking at Kafka." This piece predates all the Zuckerman novels, as well as *The Professor of Desire*, where David Kepesh dreams of a pilgrimage to the apartment of an ancient woman who claims to have been Kafka's whore. It begins with an essayistic examination of Kafka's decision, in the last year of his life, to live "apart, independent of his mother, his sisters and his father" (249). Roth quotes from Kafka's famous letter to his father to dramatize the emotional distress of a son who is spellbound before his father, who feels "the profoundest respect" for him (Kafka 45), but who is unable to act like an independent adult in the shadow of such an incredible figure of influence: "marrying is barred to me because it is your very own domain. Sometimes I imagine the map of the world spread out and you stretched diagonally across it. And I feel as if I could consider living in only those regions that either are not covered by you or are not within your reach" (Kafka 115).

Roth portrays a similar family romance – a playing out of the son's love and hatred for authority – in his depiction of the critic Milton Appel, who felt nothing but boyhood shame over the peddler's Yiddish that his father spoke (ZB 287). Zuckerman recalls his surprise when Appel, once established as a critic, applied himself to the task of editing an anthology of Yiddish fiction in his own translation (288).

A concern with the language of one's ancestors, as a revealing characteristic of their identity, returns repeatedly in *The Prague Orgy*. Zdenek appears at the outset of the novella with his Czech lover, who speaks to him in both Czech and English, excluding Zuckerman from parts of their conversation (431–2). By describing his father's reasons for writing in Yiddish, Zdenek forces Nathan to define his own Jewishness in terms of the language he speaks. "I am a Jew whose language is English" is Nathan's terse reply to his visitor's inquiry about his ability to speak the Yiddish of his forebears (432). And there is a moment of deep pathos, amidst the flurry of sardonic banter, when Zuckerman visits Zdenek's ex-wife in Prague. Even though he has persuaded Olga to give him the elder Sisovsky's stories, the manuscript remains, linguistically speaking, out of Zuckerman's reach: "I untie the ribbon on the box. Inside, hundreds of pages of unusually thick paper, rather like the heavy waxed paper that oily foodstuffs used to be wrapped in at the grocery. The ink is black, the margins perfect, the Yiddish script is sharp and neat. None of the stories seems longer than five or six pages. I can't read them" (464).

The Prague Orgy is unique among the Zuckerman books in its portrayal of a heartfelt yearning to hear the stories of the lost world of European Jewry. This patrimony brings with it not only the challenge of an unknown language, but also the question of whether the son will accept or reject his cultural inheritance; for it may prove to be an unmanageable inheritance – what Cynthia Ozick has called the "authentic bedevilment of the Europe we are heir to" (5).

Zuckerman recognizes that his imagined homeland of European culture may well be an elaborate construction, based on a yearning for a lost father, a lost identity, a lost sense of the character of the tribe. Riding a streetcar through Prague, he associates the Czech capital with the "broken city" that he imagined would be bought as a Jewish homeland with the nickels he collected as a nine-year-old for the Jewish National Fund (ZB 458). With hindsight, he realizes that the homeland he envisioned as a child was based on "emblems of pathos": antique, dilapidated homes; ever-simmering pots of cabbage soup; deep, fascinating stories dredged from a people's "infinite interest in their own existence"; and jokes, the badge of both self-mockery and fortitude in a culture busy mastering its anxiety (459).

Once he is forced to confront Olga, keeper of the Sisovskian œuvre, Zuckerman begins to question his own motivations for undertaking his odyssey of retrieval. He wonders if he is trapped in a familiar pattern of return and rebellion, a struggle between the urge to affirm and to abandon his filial love: "Is this a passionate struggle for those marvelous stories or a renewal of the struggle toward self-caricature? Still the son, still the child, in strenuous pursuit of the father's loving response? (Even when the father is Sisovsky's?) Suppose the stories aren't even marvelous" (461). Olga insists that Zuckerman is on a wild-goose chase, that his naive pursuit after great art and a murdered father is a fiasco. And it is at this point that the spectre of Bruno Schulz enters Roth's narrative most explicitly. Olga bitterly diminishes her ex-husband's tale of a murdered father to the status of a bad joke:

"And of course he told you the story of his father's death."
"He did."
"'He shot my Jew, so I shot his.'"
"Yes."
"Well that is another lie. It happened to another writer, who didn't even write in Yiddish. Who didn't have a wife or have a child." (456)

The other writer is, of course, Bruno Schulz. Unmarried. Childless. The Jew writing in a language that could never be wholly his own. The shy, burdened art teacher of Drogobych, who would not make use of the passport smuggled to him by less-timid literary colleagues, is employed by Zdenek (and Roth) to support a "useful fiction." Olga mocks Zdenek's use of this fiction. By her account the elder Sisovsky was a coward and a wastrel: "Sisovsky's father was killed in a bus accident. Sisovsky's father hid in the bathroom of a Gentile friend, hid there through the war from the Nazis, and his friend brought him cigarettes and whores" (456).[3] But Roth does not reveal Zdenek's story to be an utter lie: the recovered manuscript *is* in Yiddish, and so the reader cannot be sure how much of Zdenek's tale is true and how much is simple self-dramatization. There comes, with Olga's insistence that it is a lie, the suggestion that the thin patina of Czechness and the Yiddishist leanings ascribed to the elder Sisovsky are no more than a bogus family mythology that Zdenek has attached to the biography of Bruno Schulz.

Zuckerman himself is overwhelmed by the misdirections, the inconclusiveness, of his encounter with Olga and her candy box full of thick waxed papers. He is ultimately bedevilled by the past and ashamed of his nostalgic desire for a return to origins. The "famous, attractive, American genius" is relieved of any semblance of personal freedom (435). Upon leaving Olga's apartment with the candy box, he is confronted by the Czech secret police, who demand that he give up the Yiddish manuscript, and he is hurried out of Prague in a state limousine. He is escorted by the Czech *Kulturminister*, a mouthpiece for the worst form of authoritarian, patriarchal repression. And just as the loss of Sisovsky's manuscript to the secret police silences another "Jewish writer who might have been," so Zuckerman is reduced to childlike silence by the *Kulturminister's* tirade on "filial respect" (471). He can do no more than silently berate himself, as he is lectured to: "even if [Zdenek's] stories, those told to me in New York, were tailored to exploit the listener's sentiments, a strategically devised fiction to set me in motion, that still doesn't mitigate the sense of extraneous irrelevancy I now feel. Another assault upon a world of significance degenerating into a personal fiasco" (471).

In "'I Always Wanted You to Admire My Fasting'; or, Looking at Kafka," Roth practises an even more explicit resurrection of a literary father than that carried out in *The Prague Orgy*. Here, following the non-fiction study of Kafka's break with his family, he shifts into a fantasy about a nine-year-old Newarker, quite unpseudonymously named Philip Roth, who is taught by a distant, elegant Hebrew schoolteacher named Dr Kafka. An aborted attempt is made by the well-meaning Roths to import Kafka into the family by introducing him to a wisecracking spinster aunt. Dr Kafka's painfully uncomfortable first visit to the Roth home is almost wholly given over to a celebration of the "network of relatives" that the prospective bride boasts in America – "over two hundred and fifty people located in seven states." This "sales pitch" is intended to tempt Dr Kafka to abandon his solitary ways and join a family so rich in personal mythology that it must maintain a family newsletter and has published a book containing a "family history by 'Uncle' Lichtblau, the eighty-five-year-old patriarch of the clan"

(261). Kafka proves to be an eccentric suitor, and it seems that the odd émigré will become little Roth's uncle until the spectre of "sex" plays some mysterious havoc with the couple and the match is called off (268).

Like the tantalizing Schulz/Sisovsky conjuration in *The Prague Orgy*, Dr Kafka of the Newark Talmud Torah is one of the freakish presences constructed out of Roth's obsession with struggles – both literary and familial – between sons and father figures. In his piece on Kafka, word of the dour would-be uncle's death arrives as the elder Roth and his son are battling through what will turn up, in Roth's later work, as a prototypical Zuckermanian struggle. Now a junior at college, the independent-minded son – just beginning to develop a sense that his true patrimony may be literature and not the "blessing" of being loved in Newark – is burdened by his father's unlimited approbation (268–9). In *The Prague Orgy* this predicament still haunts Nathan Zuckerman, even with his father dead. The contradictory desire for both allegiance and independence is aroused by the "strategically devised fiction" of Zdenek Sisovsky (471), and the difficulty of reconciling these two urges is depicted – almost lampooned – as the famous American son is shipped like a baby back to his homeland.

Behind Roth's epilogue to the Zuckerman Trilogy, we might place as a backdrop a lyrical piece by Bruno Schulz, which offers an eloquent explanation of the urge to come up with marvelous variations on one's family tree. Schulz had been asked, as Roth has been throughout his career, to justify his continual need to return to concerns of origin and inheritance. The necessity of such a literary agenda, Schulz argued, rises out of the desire to uncover "a genealogy *par excellence* [which] follows the spiritual family tree down to those depths where it merges into mythology, to be lost in the mutterings of mythological delirium. I have always felt that the roots of the individual spirit, traced far enough down, would be lost in some matrix of myth. This is the ultimate depth; it is impossible to reach farther down" (Ficowski, *Letters* 114).

5 Philip Roth's Literary Ghost: Rereading Anne Frank

Philip Roth's *The Ghost Writer* has been looked upon as one of the author's scandals. Its presentation of Anne Frank as a survivor, miraculously saved from death at Bergen-Belsen, led one critic to characterize the novel as a prime example of artistic "falsification of the Holocaust" for personal gain and as a work that "fails to make an honest attempt to follow the known historical record" of events (Shatzky 107, 110).[1] Reviewers were also uneasy with Roth's use of his fiction regarding Anne Frank to examine his own writing life; it is his alter ego, Nathan Zuckerman, who imagines her alive after the war, surmising that a young woman whom he meets at the Berkshire home of a well-known Jewish writer is the famous victim of the Nazis. Regarding this thematic turn one reviewer, who was otherwise enthusiastic about the novel, admitted to feeling "slightly cheated, slightly offended" upon sensing the outcome of Roth's use of Anne Frank (Towers 13). Another largely laudatory review singled it out as "no more than a conceit," an effort at getting a laugh from the prospect of "Philip Roth, the scourge of the literary rabbis, marrying *the* Anne" (Beatty 39).

With these responses as a starting point, I would like to consider *The Ghost Writer* as an important effort at examining the way in which aspects of the Holocaust have been received by a variety of audiences since the Second World War. I will argue that an important consideration for Roth is to review the way in which the diary of Anne Frank has been received and to revise drastically the popular perception of its writer. While pursuing this end, Roth considers how the claims of Jewish identity and history have affected his own writing life. Attention to communities of readers, those of our own era and of the past, allows us, in the words of Marcel Proust, to "see the universe with the eyes of another" (179). Such an approach posits an ethical relationship between readers, calling for an attention to many readings and for a regard for the way that readings at different times contribute to the development of meaning. In Hans Jauss's words, this approach places "problems of interhuman communication" at the centre of "attempts toward a theory of literature's reception" ("Interview" 86).[2]

Studies of literature dealing with the Holocaust call for a particularly vigilant attention to the way in which artistic productions engage with political, philosophical, and ethical questions raised by the Nazi genocide. Although writing about the Holocaust must contend with the aesthetic problems of representing terrible events, as readers we cannot escape the pressing demand that we take into account the relationship between literature and society, and contend with the ability of texts to engage with the broader contexts within which they are produced.

It is worth noting that a number of reviewers gave Roth's treatment of Anne Frank only cursory consideration and concentrated on the novel as a self-reflexive *Bildungs*-cum-*Künstlerroman* with Nathan Zuckerman as its thinly veiled autobiographical protagonist. The reviewer in *Commonweal* suggested that the novel focused on the question of how one is "to live and serve one's talent purely and uncompromisingly in a world which has its own and very different ideas of what is important and valuable" (Maloff 628). *Time's* reviewer noted that *The Ghost Writer* "debunks romantic notions of the writing life" (Sheppard 70), and in the *New York Times Book Review*, Robert Towers centred his commentary on "the tension between 'pure' art and 'messy life'" (13).

It is true that the novel begins as Nathan recalls himself at "twenty-three, writing and publishing [his] first short stories, and like many a *Bildungsroman* hero before," already contemplating his "own massive *Bildungsroman*" (1). This is, however, only the novel's point of departure and not its ultimate focus. By insisting that *The Ghost Writer's* most pressing theme is the pursuit of "pure" art, or the related prospect of serving one's talent "uncompromisingly," readers have responded to Roth's narrative as a parable about artistic yearning, a witty *roman-à-clef*. I will argue, however, that he encourages us to read his novel through terms that include, but are not limited to, such purely literary concerns. Rather than presenting the possibility of artistic production, unencumbered and remote from the "messiness" of life, *The Ghost Writer* invites us to recognize how a narrative presents its readers with a "cultural artifact," which is created, in Stephen Greenblatt's words, out of the "zone of social transaction" in which the work is produced and received by a variety of reading communities (*Learning* 3, 11). Greenblatt explains how literary criticism might more fruitfully examine this zone: "We need to develop terms to describe the ways in which material – here official documents, private papers, newspaper clippings, and so forth – is transferred from one discursive sphere to another and becomes aesthetic property" (*Learning* 157).

To exemplify the workings of this process Greenblatt recounts how the biography of a Texas murderer prompted Norman Mailer to write his "true life novel" *The Executioner's Song*. The novel's popularity led another convict, Jack H. Abbott, to contact Mailer, who helped Abbott gain parole and supported the publication of his prison writings, *In the Belly of the Beast*. Shortly after being paroled Abbott committed a highly publicized murder in Manhattan that in turn provided the material for a successful play (Greenblatt, *Learning* 156–7). I describe these events and their treatment in a variety of literary venues because it is just such an "unsettling circulation of materials and discourses" that has resulted from the post-war popularity of Anne Frank's diary.

It is, as I will show, her own writing, her day-to-day descriptions of her life in hiding, and the desire to recover the initial intent and voice of her diary that prompt Roth to embroider Zuckerman's fantasy. But it is the history of the diary's reception – an attention to its "communities of readers," as Jauss puts it – that informs his approach to the diary's legacy. Roth sets out to "read all the textual traces of the past" that have appeared as Anne Frank's voice and character have been resurrected on Broadway, as part of the post-war debates concerning Jewish communal and political commitment, and in the imaginations of post-war writers who appreciate the diary as literature (Greenblatt, *Learning* 14).

We might, at the outset, characterize the distinctively American stage on which Roth sets his fiction. *The Ghost Writer* begins in 1956, four years after Otto Frank secured an American publication of a selection from his daughter's diary under the title *Anne Frank: The Diary of a Young Girl* (CE 74).[3] An extremely enthusiastic review in the *New York Times* by Meyer Levin helped to bring the diary immediate success in America; a Broadway play written by Frances Goodrich and Albert Hackett opened to overwhelmingly laudatory reviews in October 1955 and went on to win a Pulitzer Prize (CE 80). By setting Nathan's visit to the home of his hero, the writer E.I. Lonoff, in the winter of 1956, Roth carefully situates his narrative at a point when Anne Frank and the play about her were an American cause célèbre. A lengthy conflict was underway at the time between Meyer Levin and the writers of the Broadway play, who had secured the support of Otto Frank. I will return to these events later, for Levin's increasingly public struggle and the concern he had for what he called the Goodrich-Hackett play's "programmatic, politicized dilution of the Jewish tragedy" bear important similarities to Nathan's criticism of the insular concerns of his community and may have influenced Roth's conception of this part of his narrative (Levin, *Obsession* 30). When we keep this historical perspective in mind, the loosely connected sections of *The Ghost Writer* take on clear thematic unity.

As the narrative progresses through Nathan's encounter with Lonoff, his fight with his father over his fiction, his musings about Amy Bellette actually being Anne Frank, to the point at which he writes the fanciful "Femme Fatale," he confronts different aspects of what will become a lifelong predicament: an experience of "disinheritance from those he must write about" combined with a "responsibility to their history" (H. Lee 70). The novel stages a conflict of attachment and resistance to the figures who have most influenced him that is typical of Zuckerman. His adulation of Lonoff as an inheritor of the mantle of Isaac Babel is diminished as he views the man's odd, seemingly bloodless existence in the desolate winter setting of the Berkshires. The struggle between Nathan, his family, and the Jewish worthies of Newark is based on their disagreement over how Jewish life in America should be represented. And "Femme Fatale," the most provocative section of the novel, focuses Nathan's (and Roth's) concerns with communal responsibility and Jewish literary heritage and history by examining the legacy of Anne Frank.

As Nathan deals with his ambivalent feelings about Jewish identity and community, he criticizes the timidity of American Jewry in the 1950s and their deeply felt desire for acceptance. His father warns him that the "one thing" that his satiric fictions will arouse in Gentiles is a dislike of "[k]ikes and their love of money" (94). The informal committee of censors that condemns Nathan's story "Higher Education" – Judge Leopold Wapter, his wife, and Nathan's father – represents the stifling conformity of mainstream American Jewry in the fifties.[4] The exasperation that Nathan feels is based not so much on innate rebelliousness, or even on his belief in the higher demands of art, as on his perception that his critics show a hypocritical refusal to accept *any* unorthodox view of Jewish communal life. At the heart of this hypocrisy, as Nathan sees it, is the general sense of siege and mistrust that derives from the community's vestigial, even guilty, identification with the victims of the Holocaust. Newark Jews still view themselves as vulnerable to anti-Semitic attacks, which they associate with those on Jews in Germany before the war and during the Holocaust.

These issues are raised in a telephone conversation between Nathan and his mother concerning the criticism levelled at his fiction by Judge Wapter, who is, according to Nathan, Newark's third "most admired Jew" (96). Nathan's mother begs him to answer the judge's letter, a high-toned dismissal of "Higher Education" that includes such queries as "If you had been living in Nazi Germany in the thirties, would you have written such a story? ... Can you honestly say that there is anything in your short story that would not warm the heart of a Julius Streicher or a Joseph Goebbels?" And in a postscript, the judge "strongly" advises Nathan to see "the Broadway production of *The Diary of Anne Frank* ... [an] unforgettable experience" (102–4). Exasperated, Nathan criticizes his mother's respect for Judge Wapter, shouting,

"The Big Three, Mama! Streicher, Goebbels, and your son! What about the *judge's* humility? Where's *his* modesty?"

"He only meant that what happened to the Jews –"

"In Europe – not in Newark! We are not the wretched of Belsen! We were not the victims of that crime!"

"But we *could* be – in their place we *would* be. Nathan, violence is nothing new to Jews, you *know* that!" (106)

Nathan's sense of the disparity between his view of the position of Jews in the United States and that of his parents is emphasized by his memories of feeling deeply at home in Newark. Walking through his childhood neighbourhood, he says:

There was no end to all I could remember happening to me on this street of one-family brick houses more or less like ours, owned by Jews more or less like us ...

... sometimes it seemed to me that there were more Zuckermans in Newark than Negroes. I wouldn't see as many of them in a year as I saw cousins on an ordinary Sunday driving around the city with my father. (88–9)

In an interview published two years after the appearance of *The Ghost Writer*, Roth lends texture to this portrait of his own upbringing on the Jewish streets of Newark:

I had simultaneously been surrounded from birth with a *definition* of the Jew of such stunning emotional and historical proportions that I couldn't but be enveloped by it, contrary though it was to my own experience. This was the definition of the Jew as sufferer, the Jew as object of ridicule, disgust, scorn, contempt, derision, of every heinous form of persecution and brutality, including murder. If the definition was not supported by my own experience, it surely was by the experience of my grandparents and their forebears, and by the experience of our European contemporaries. The disparity between this tragic dimension of Jewish life in Europe and the actualities of our daily lives as Jews in New Jersey was something that I had to puzzle over. ("Ghosts" 128)

Roth's young alter ego is accordingly exasperated by the refusal of Wapter and his father to differentiate between post-war America and the "old country," especially Europe under Hitler, as well as by their inability to accept what he believes is an objective view of their community. In his letter to Nathan, Judge Wapter writes of Anne Frank as an exemplary and cautionary figure in the tradition of Jewish suffering. He and his wife use restrictive, moralistic terms, questioning Nathan's "credentials" for writing about Jewish life. Do the characters in his story, they ask, "represent a fair sample of the kinds of people that make up a typical contemporary community of Jews?" And they snidely point out that "Higher Education" may make money for Nathan rather than furthering "the well-being of the Jewish people" (103).

Blinded by self-important smugness and conformity, Judge Wapter refuses to recognize that the questions which he puts to Nathan could well have been asked of Anne Frank herself. The Franks were by no means "experts" on Jewish culture, and Anne's diary, with its characters limited to the eight inmates of the "annexe," offers nothing like a representative sample of Jewish life. In fact, it portrays assimilated, well-off Dutch families much influenced by the culture of Germany. And of course, Anne was thinking not of Jewish empowerment but of her own ambition and interests when she wrote, "Just imagine how interesting it would be if I were to publish a romance of the 'Secret Annexe.' The title alone would be enough to think it was a detective story" (CE 60; *Diary* 211–12).

It is not Nathan but his elders who raise Anne as an iconic figure, creating a fiction about her that serves their own purposes. The source of their interest in her experience is not the diary itself but a Broadway play based upon it. Nathan differs with his elders even over how one should become acquainted with the Franks' history. Now living in Manhattan, he dismisses the play, performed a quick bus ride from his "five-flight Village walk-up": "I didn't see it. I read the book" (38, 107). By recommending the play and speaking of his pleasure at seeing its opening production, Judge Wapter cites the Goodrich-Hackett dramatization of the diary as an appropriate literary response to the Holocaust. Implicit in Nathan's disdain for this version is his sense that the play has silenced Anne and the ambiguity of her views, effectively putting her ghost to rest.

The Broadway play is indeed worth examining for its faults and ambiguities. Its social impact, little more than a decade after Anne Frank's death, was unquestionable. The bulk of the reviews that it received ranged "from good to very good"; the actors and the director, as well as the authors, went on to win various awards; it was staged in Sweden, the Netherlands, and throughout Germany, as well as in Israel (CE 80). Among its Jewish viewers the feeling was that the play was "'doing good' for the Jews" and "arousing sympathy" (Levin, *Obsession* 127). There were, however, notable exceptions. A scathing review in *Commentary* argued that the playwrights had neglected to listen "to the *inner* voice of Anne Frank … the true voice of the diary," opting instead for an approximation of a precocious American adolescent – a creature "not to be taken seriously" (Ballif 464–5). The *Commentary* reviewer was also critical of the playwrights' insertion of actions "for the sake of dramatic situation," subverting the play's claims to be an honest representation of the diary. Worst among these, according to Ballif, was the cliché-ridden courtship scene between Anne and Peter Van Daan, which "has virtually nothing to do with" the diary (465).

The *Commonweal's* reviewer ended his criticism of the play with a vision, prescient of Roth's novel, of Anne, having seen the production herself, rushing home to pencil her own review: "Oh no, they have gotten it all wrong. It wasn't that way at all" ("Songs" 92). Meyer Levin, with his characteristic interest in intrigue and the ever-present threat of "political culture-control" (*Anne* ii), wrote that amid the din of acclaim among Jews and the public at large, "an intellectual snob dared to say the show was full of *kitsch*; now and again a rabbi, almost in secret, would admit he thought it bad" (*Obsession* 127). Levin remained resentful that his own dramatization of the diary had been rejected, and he records a lengthy list of people who preferred his version to the Goodrich-Hackett piece. Among these were Albert Camus and Elie Wiesel; the latter wrote to Levin saying that he "would gladly and willingly do whatever possible to put back Anne Frank in her true light" (*Obsession* 29).

Levin's involvement in what he calls the Anne Frank "trouble" reached back to his contact with Otto Frank in the early fifties, when he helped to arrange for the English-language publication of *The Diary of a Young Girl* (*Obsession* 7–8). Before the Diary appeared, he also arranged for it to be serialized in *Commentary* (*Obsession* 44). Following the book's success, his suggestion that it be made into a play was at first rebuffed by Otto Frank, but Levin offered a script that Frank later accepted, commenting, according to Levin, "I cannot imagine how anyone could write the characters more truly" (*Obsession* 69–70). By a combination of coincidence, circumstance, and show-business pressures depicted in Levin's memoir *The Obsession* (1973), his version was rejected and replaced, after a good deal of legal wrangling, by the text written by Goodrich and Hackett.

There is no need to dwell here on Levin's theories about why his play was "suppressed," but his appraisal of the two different theatrical renderings of the diary is relevant (*Anne* i).[5] His key criticism of the Broadway play is that its authors left out the "very quality of the Diary as a document of the Jewish disaster. Every Jew who had died in the Holocaust was misrepresented" (*Obsession* 124).[6] Levin believed that his play was seen to be "too Jewish" (9) and that producers, as well as Otto Frank, did not want the diary portrayed as a work that brought "home the Holocaust" experience "in its Jewish essence" (28–9).[7] Broadway producers and investors, many of them Jews, supported instead what Levin describes as a piece of moralizing propaganda with a broadly "universalist" and humanist perspective, which diluted the Jewishness of the characters and the particularity of their experience (65).

Levin's assertions are confirmed by my own reading of the Broadway play, in which the resonant line, twice repeated, is "I still believe, in spite of everything, that people are really good at heart" (168, 174). This comment, found in the diary entry dated 15 July 1944, is embedded by Goodrich and Hackett in an earnest speech of which there is no trace in Anne's own text. Addressing Peter Van Daan, she announces: "Oh, I don't mean you have to be Orthodox … or believe in heaven and hell and purgatory and things … I just mean some religion … it doesn't matter what" (167–8). She goes on to say: "We're not the only people that've had to suffer. There've always been people that've had to … sometimes one race … sometimes another" (168).

If these feelings were expressed in the diary – by no means feelings to dismiss in a fifteen-year-old girl – one could not quarrel with the play's intentions. But Levin and others have placed alongside these sentiments the words that Anne actually set down in her diary:

Who has made us Jews different from all other people? Who has allowed us to suffer so terribly up till now? It is God that has made us as we are, but it will be God, too, who will raise us up again. If we bear all this suffering and if there are still Jews left, when it is over, then Jews, instead of being doomed, will be held up as an example. Who knows, it might even be our religion from which the world and all peoples learn good, and for that reason and that reason only do we have to suffer now. We can never become just Netherlanders, or just English, or … representatives of any other country for that matter, we will always remain Jews, but we want to, too. (*Obsession* 29–30; *Diary* 228)

Elsewhere Anne writes against any facile affirmation of essential human goodness: "I don't believe that the big men, the politicians and the capitalists alone, are guilty of the war. Oh no, the little man is just as guilty, otherwise the peoples of the world would have risen long ago! There's in people simply an urge to destroy, an urge to kill, to murder and rage" (*Diary* 244–5).

Anne herself does not equivocate or hesitate, nor does she reach for the banal truism that all people suffer. The objects in which the Broadway Anne recognizes a spiritual glow – "the trees ... and flowers ... and seagulls" – are reminiscent of fairy tales (Goodrich and Hackett 168). Such childlike ideas, which could easily be the expression of a sheltered, unselfconscious imagination, avoid any consideration of how Anne Frank's notes to herself did in fact include questions about the particular Jewish character of her fate. Such considerations arise most notably in her rhetorical question about Jewish suffering and in her sense that this suffering may be part of a divine scheme for the moral education of humanity. More to the point, the voice of the diary communicates a particular identity and character that is not conveyed by the voice given to Anne by Goodrich and Hackett. The Broadway character expresses herself in bland ineffectual language transformed by translation and a lack of any true empathy with its source. Algene Ballif wrote in *Commentary* of Anne's Broadway voice as one "without nuance" that "rises and falls in set cadence," peppered with "incoherent halts [that] serve only to heighten the effect of superficiality and inarticulateness" (464).

The move toward universalization of the events recorded in the diary is furthered in the play's foreword, which was written by the theatre critic Brooks Atkinson. "Fundamentally," he says, the diary "is a portrait of adolescence" (ix). This move away from the particulars of the Franks' experience is further supported in the stage directions, where Otto Frank is introduced as a "gentle, cultured European in his middle years" (4). Like Arthur Miller's salesman, Frank is presented as a Jew whose Jewishness is purposefully obscured. The play's use of Chanukah as the one Jewish ritual that the Franks are seen to observe is intriguing in the same vein; in the diary Anne mentions Yom Kippur and other solemn Jewish occasions (CE 237). In North America, Chanukah has become accepted as a kind of Jewish Christmas. Anne notes in the diary that her father's Chanukah gift to her was a copy of the New Testament, and this detail, retained in the play, signals to the audience that they need not make much of the Franks' Jewishness. Her speech in which she tells Peter that he does not have to "believe in heaven and hell and purgatory and things" reinforces this bias. These notions are so patently, but blandly Christian that one has difficulty imagining them being invoked with such earnestness by a Jew, however assimilated.

The Yiddish expressions in the play are few and seem forced. Mr Frank's "Locheim" (To life!) over a "glass of cognac" seems unlikely (161), and the stage direction suggesting the proper pronunciation of "amen" as "O-mayn" may be intended to make up for the conspicuous absence in the script of Jewish content (84). Equally removed and foreign to the ear is a translation of a traditional Chanukah song as "Oh Hanukkah! Oh Hanukkah! The sweet celebration" (96). This awkward rendering of the Yiddish – *Chanukah, oy Chanukah, a yom tov a sheiner* – was inserted when Garson Kanin, the play's director, overruled the writers' choice of "Rock of Ages" as a concluding song, arguing that it would close the first act on a note "as flat as a latke" (Graver 90).

With the Chanukah scene as the single, half-hearted effort at depicting the Franks as Jews, the play seems designed to confirm Atkinson's view of Anne's account of her years in the "annexe" as a "portrait of adolescence." Kanin reinforced this tendency to play down her Jewishness, arguing that the "fact that in this play the symbols of persecution and oppression are Jews is incidental." For him, Anne's story was first and foremost an "exalting comment on the human spirit" (qtd. in Graver 89). The diary *is* a portrait of a young girl's struggle to come to terms with her own coming of age, her relationship with her parents, and her attitudes toward the way that the adult world impinges on the desire of youth for freedom. But our knowledge of Anne Frank's fate, of the curtailment of her complicated adolescence, makes her experience emblematic of the Holocaust and the "millions of unlived lives robbed from the murdered Jews" (Roth, *Ghost Writer*, 1979 ed., 150). In the most troublesome expression of its bland theme, the play's conclusion implies that the capture of the Franks by the Germans cannot threaten Anne's new-found independence and maturity: "ANNE stands, holding her school satchel, looking over at her father and mother with a soft, reassuring smile. She is no longer a child, but a woman with courage to meet whatever lies ahead" (170). The photographs taken at Bergen-Belsen shortly after its liberation, of twisted, brutalized forms still bearing expressions of suffering, conclusively challenge the distressing banalization in this passage of the actual horror suffered by Anne.

Levin condemns the Goodrich-Hackett play for its complicity in the "process of image deformation and of the subtle manipulation of ideas in the public mind" (*Obsession* 32). Apart from commercial considerations, the authors, it would seem, saw their play as a balm or cure for the trauma of Anne's death. The claim that "people are really good at heart" and the play's final scene portraying her father as a survivor of Auschwitz who has undergone a "great change" and is now "calm" urge the audience to unburden themselves of the pain of the Holocaust. The authors act – as has been said of some contemporary Jewish and Christian theologians – as if the Holocaust did not happen. This fantasy is supported by recourse to pre-war sentiments, offered in a context that is seemingly untouched by the worst of Nazi abuse and violence. At the play's conclusion, Otto Frank, the "gentle, cultured European," closes the book on his past, as if his daughter's indomitable strength makes up for the destruction of the Jews of Europe. Bound in the play's moralistic constraints, Anne Frank becomes an oddly stereotypical character: a precocious, talkative Pollyanna speaking for all that is good in the world. Given its focus on the goodness of people and Otto Frank's serenity after his return from the camps, the Nazis can be written out of history, and Anne's "soft, reassuring smile" can ease the discomfort that one feels over the ugliness of genocide. As Bruno Bettelheim wrote in 1960, the play "encourages us" to ignore the implications of Auschwitz: "If all men are good at heart, there never really was an Auschwitz, nor is there any possibility that it may recur" (251).

In an article entitled "The American History of Anne Frank's Diary," Judith Doneson explains the play's tendency to universalize the Holocaust by placing it in the context of post-war American political and social trends. In the shadow of the witch hunts organized by Joseph McCarthy's House Committee on Un-American Activities, conformity and assimilation became imperatives for those who wished to be seen as good Americans. At the same time, with the decline of anti-Semitism following the war, Jewish public life was infused with a desire to "conform to the existing principles of the day, to try not to 'stand out'" (Doneson 152). The public virtues of the 1950s, proposing "Americanization" as the ultimate goal for minorities, along with the desire – felt, it seems, by the play's authors and producer, by Otto Frank, and by such interested parties as Lillian Hellman – that it reach the widest possible audience, ensured that Anne's European Jewish experiences would be filtered through an assimilationist American outlook (Doneson 152–4). As it moved from the page to the stage and eventually to the screen, the diary passed like a whispered message around a circle of strangers and was fundamentally transformed.[8]

The "Americanization" of the Holocaust is as timely an issue today as it was in the wake of the diary's popularity, as critics and film-goers argue over the merits of what James Young has called two "gigantic institutions" – the Holocaust Memorial Museum in Washington and Steven Spielberg's *Schindler's List*. Both have been criticized for offering a markedly American-centred representation of the experience of the Nazis' victims.[9] The threat, then, of a "programmatic, political dilution of the Jewish tragedy" is very much alive. In the case of Anne Frank, the urge to universalize her experience and Americanize her character may have made her story palatable to a wide and diverse audience, but the effects of such popularization of the Holocaust are deep and troubling.

Jonathan and Daniel Boyarin, in a provocative essay examining Jewish identity in light of the Holocaust and the existence of the state of Israel, point to some of the more sinister characteristics of the universalist creed. Though universalism is often said to ensure a "liberal and benevolent" response to other exclusionary or particularist systems, they point out that it can also become "a powerful force for coercive discourses of sameness, denying ... the rights of Jews, women, and others to retain their difference" (707). When considered in this light, such political and social tendencies, no matter how well intentioned, bear an uncanny resemblance to the tenets of Hitlerism, which fanatically denied the rights of any groups in society said to be contrary to the Germanic "ideal."

Roth's decision to set *The Ghost Writer* in 1956, when the play about Anne Frank reigned triumphant, must be seen as a deft rhetorical response to what he views as the assimilationist outlook within which the Jewish community in America chose to inscribe recent European history. There is much more at stake than the nature of artistic freedom as Nathan challenges community consensus, shouting, "I am on my own!" (109).

Through the inspired fantasy that he concocts in "Femme Fatale," Nathan himself reveals a very personal relationship with the memory of Anne. The fiction that he writes during his sleepless night in Lonoff's study – after straining to hear his host arguing upstairs with Amy Bellette, the young woman he imagines is Anne – reveals an intimate knowledge of the diary and its author. Such knowledge, clearly based on serious research and reflection, puts

Nathan's fictionalized treatment of Anne in a rather singular light. The crux of the fiction is the premise that Amy Bellette, who is helping Lonoff edit his manuscripts, is actually Anne Frank. Having survived the war, she lives under an assumed name as one of the many "displaced persons" who rebuilt their lives in America. Amy reveals that in 1945 she was sixteen, making her twenty-seven in 1956; as Nathan notes, she is "Anne Frank's age exactly" (168). (Born on 12 June 1929, Anne would have been twenty-seven in the winter of 1956 [CE 3].)

There are other signs in *The Ghost Writer* of Roth's care in getting such details right. "[O]nly a year earlier" – that is in late 1955 – Nathan's "femme fatale" visited the opening of the Broadway play based on her diary (122); the play indeed opened at the Cort Theatre on 5 October 1955 (Goodrich and Hackett xiii). And just as the details relating to Anne's birth are correct, so the version that Nathan's Anne tells of her reported death is true to the historical record. Anne's travel from the Dutch transit camp at Westerbork to Auschwitz has been verified by train records (*Anne Frank in the World* 207), but her journey from Auschwitz to Belsen and her existence and death there have been confirmed by a reconstruction of the patterns of transport from Auschwitz in late 1945 and by numerous eyewitness accounts of inmates at both camps (CE 52–3). Nathan is accurate, then, when his Anne reports being shipped to Auschwitz sometime in October (128). Haary Paape, in the critical edition of the diary, pinpoints three transports – on 28 October and 1 and 2 November – one of which most likely took Anne and her sister Margot to Bergen-Belsen (52). Nathan refers to inmates who "claimed to have seen her dead of typhus" (1979 ed., 128; CE 54).

He is also accurate in his account of Anne's family's worsening circumstances in the summer of 1942, presenting it as he imagines Amy/Anne would narrate it to Lonoff, but embellishing it as well with a wealth of historical detail:

In July of 1942, some two years after the beginning of the Nazi occupation, [Otto Frank] had taken his wife and his two young daughters into hiding. Along with another Jewish family, the Franks lived safely for twenty-five months …

… Of the eight who'd been together in the sealed-off attic rooms, only Otto Frank survived the concentration camps. When he came back to Amsterdam after the war, the Dutch family who had been their protectors gave him the notebooks that had been kept in hiding by his younger daughter,[10] a girl of fifteen when she died in Belsen: a diary, some ledgers she wrote in, and a sheaf of papers emptied out of her briefcase when the Nazis were ransacking the place for valuables.[11] Frank printed and circulated the diary only privately at first,[12] as a memorial to his family, but in 1947 it was published in a regular edition under the title *Het Achterhuis* – "The House Behind." (126–7)

The Franks did go into hiding in July of 1942 (*Diary* 26); their hiding place was discovered in August 1944, after what they suspected was the denunciation by a workman in the warehouse below the "annexe" (*CE* 21, 28). Thus all the details that Nathan gives in his fiction regarding Anne Frank are scrupulously accurate.

In light of Roth's reliable and careful use of the documentary evidence, we must ask what the effect is of his fictional revival of Anne Frank and how the Holocaust figures in his efforts to reconstitute a Jewish identity. The reviewers whom I have quoted do not consider *The Ghost Writer* to be a novel primarily about the Holocaust, nor do they see it as an examination of Anne Frank's legacy. But "Femme Fatale" can be viewed as a satisfying response to the dilemmas of filial, communal, and literary identification, as well as a thoroughgoing response to many of the concerns related to the representation of the Holocaust.

As I have noted, the reviewers' appraisal of the novel as a *Bildungsroman* is not unfounded, nor is their interest in the novel as an apparent *roman-à-clef*, with characters reminiscent of Saul Bellow, Bernard Malamud, and of course the young Roth. But the most compelling element of Zuckerman's search for a literary heritage focuses, not on the writings of E.I. Lonoff, but on those of Anne Frank. Although Nathan reveres Lonoff and his stories "about wandering Jews" and their melancholy lives, his weekend in the Berkshires with "the region's most original storyteller since Melville and Hawthorne" does not amount to a celebratory meeting of kindred spirits (4, 11). Nathan is an amorous hedonist who does not hesitate to drag girls "onto the floor" of his apartment while his ballerina girlfriend is "safely off dancing her heart out" (36).

By contrast, the middle-aged Lonoff strikes Nathan as a "literary ascetic" (10), a famous man acting like "a nobody from nowhere" (14), living in a house surrounded by "the bare limbs of big dark maple trees and fields of driven snow. Purity. Serenity. Simplicity.

Seclusion. All one's concentration and flamboyance and originality reserved for the grueling, exalted, transcendent calling" (5). Though he envies Lonoff's talent and repose, Nathan has fashioned for himself an identity, after the model of Isaac Babel, as a Jew with spectacles on his nose, autumn in his heart, and "blood in his penis" (49). Lonoff, despite his Babel-like stories, has made a life out of diminishing the effects of the last term in this triad. And ultimately, Nathan sees his idol for what he has become: an aging man in a sterile marriage who refuses to forsake his disappointing life for a chance at personal happiness because of his self-perceived "singularity" (71). To Nathan's query over why he does not go abroad with the companion he desires, the elder writer retorts, "Like the fat lady said about the polka-dot dress, 'It's nice, but it's not Lonoff'" (70).

As the unpleasantness in Lonoff's personal life is revealed, his problems become a backdrop for Nathan's thoughts about his own literary and familial responsibilities. In the end, it is not America's "most famous literary ascetic" who helps him master these responsibilities, but Anne Frank, whose experience and example best represent a site of identification for the young writer as he looks for his place in the world (10). In the course of "Femme Fatale" she is reconstituted not as a mere ghost, but as one of the most widely read Jewish writers of her time. Nathan imagines her surviving Belsen to begin an anonymous American adolescence, in which she resolves "not to speak about what she had been through" (130). But the accidental discovery that her father is alive and that her diary has become an international success alters her ambitions. She can no longer view herself, with uncomplicated pride, as an attractive coed with a "remarkable prose style" whose past has been completely buried (28). Upon first looking into the Dutch version of *Het Achterhuis* she cannot resist correcting passages that ring as "decorative" or "unclear," but overall she regards her work with pleasure: "mostly she marked passages she couldn't believe that she had written as little more than a child. Why, what eloquence, Anne – it gave her gooseflesh, whispering her own name in Boston – what deftness, what wit! How nice, she thought, if I could write like this for Mr. Lonoff's English 12. 'It's good,' she heard him saying, 'it's the best thing you've ever done, Miss Bellette'" (136).

Roth reminds us that this vision of Anne Frank as a writer – and not as simply a charming child who recorded terrible circumstances – has long been in the public record as part of her diary: "I must work," she wrote, "so as not to be a fool, to get on, to become a journalist, because that's what I want! I know that I *can* write, a couple of my stories are good, my descriptions of the 'Secret Annexe' are humorous, there's a lot in my diary that speaks – whether I have real talent remains to be seen" (CE 60; *Diary* 4 April 1944). "Of course," Nathan says, "it had eventually to occur to any child so *mad on books and reading* that for all she knew she was writing a book of her own" (137). Roth also quotes from the diary entry dated 11 May 1944, in which Anne states that her "greatest wish is to become a journalist someday and later on a famous writer" (1979 ed., 138; *Diary* 255).

These aspirations are notably absent from the Broadway play; similarly, reviewers of *The Ghost Writer* have not emphasized Roth's interest in this aspect of Anne Frank's writings. Nathan's Anne – mature, sophisticated, ambitious – puts some of the more sentimental sections of her diary into a post-war context, reconsidering them with the critical eye of a self-conscious practising writer: "She was not, after all, the fifteen-year-old who could, while hiding from a holocaust, tell Kitty, *I still believe that people are really good at heart.* Her youthful ideals had suffered no less than she had in the windowless freight car from Westerbork and in the barracks at Auschwitz and on the Belsen heath. She had not come to hate the human race for what it was – what could it be but what it was? – but she did not feel seemly anymore singing its praises" (146).

Here Roth provides a subtle, but severe corrective to the questionable humanism of the Goodrich-Hackett play. He portrays as well Anne's recognition that her diary is oddly lacking in overt Jewish reference and in many ways unsuited to becoming one of the archetypal texts of literature about the Holocaust. I will quote Nathan's depiction of Anne at length in an effort to convey his (and of course Roth's) sense of the diary's character:

All her reasoning, all her fantastical thinking about the ordained mission of her book followed from this: neither she nor her parents came through in the diary as anything like representative of religious or observant Jews. Her mother lit candles on Friday night and that was about the extent of it. As for celebrations, she had found St. Nicholas's Day, once she'd been introduced to it in hiding, much more fun than Chanukah, and along with Pim made all kinds of clever gifts and even written a Santa Claus poem to enliven the festivities. When Pim settled upon a children's Bible as her present for the holiday – so she might learn something about the New Testament – Margot hadn't approved. Margot's ambition was to be a mid-wife in Palestine. She was the only one of them who seemed to have given serious thought to religion. The diary that Margot kept, had it ever been found, would not have been quite so sparing as hers in curiosity about Judaism, or plans for leading a Jewish life. Certainly it was impossible for her to imagine Margot thinking, let alone writing with longing in her diary, *the time will come when we are people again, and not just Jews.*

She had written these words, to be sure, still suffering the aftereffects of a nighttime burglary in the downstairs warehouse. The burglary had seemed certain to precipitate their discovery by the police, and for days afterward everyone was weak with terror. And for her, along with the residue of fear and the dubious sense of relief, there was, of course, the guilt-tinged bafflement when she realized that, unlike Lies, she had again been spared. In the aftermath of that gruesome night, she went around and around trying to understand the meaning of their persecution, one moment writing about the misery of being Jews and only Jews to their enemies, and then in the next airily wondering if *it might even be our religion from which the world and all peoples learn good … We can never become just Netherlanders,* she reminded Kitty, *we will always remain Jews, but we want to, too.* (142–3)

This passage bristles with honesty and accuracy. "Femme Fatale" portrays a mind divided, through its depiction of a young woman who thinks of herself as Jewish but can also readily see that her allegiances and interests do not always lead her to live a life that could be viewed as "representative." There are no universalizing platitudes here. Amy/Anne's perception of her experience is grounded in the actual Anne's acceptance of the particularity of her youthful fate, as well as in her unwavering, but unsentimental acceptance of Jewish identity, with its complexity and struggles: "*it might even be our religion from which the world and all peoples learn good … We will always remain Jews, but we want to, too*" (143). These words, omitted, as Levin emphasizes, from the Broadway play, are fore-grounded by Roth, who thus attempts to put "back Anne Frank in her true light," as Wiesel wanted to do after viewing the Broadway play (*Obsession* 29–30).

By imagining an American life for Amy/Anne, Nathan avoids confusing his own experiences in post-war New England with those of the Jews during the Holocaust; his fictional Anne is well aware of how fully *remade* she is, fit and adjusted to the demands of Ivy

League college life. And yet it is the historical Anne – her youthful writerly yearnings, her terrible experiences, and the particularity of her voice – that proves so meaningful to Nathan. By transplanting Anne Frank into Zuckerman's imaginative world, Roth can more directly reveal how the singular qualities of her life and writing might serve as touchstones for an American writer.

Through Nathan's reconsideration of Anne's life, actual and imagined, Roth considers the effect that a book such as the diary can have and on what terms a writer like himself, removed from the Holocaust, can build a sense of connection with the dead. In Amy/Anne's appraisal, the Franks' assimilated character is a fortuitous element in the diary's portrait of Jewish life. The lesson that can be learned from this, she says, is how little it took to make the Franks "the enemy": "How could even the most obtuse of the ordinary ignore what had been done to the Jews *just for being Jews*, how could even the most benighted of the Gentiles fail to get the idea when they read in *Het Achterhuis* that once a year the Franks sang a harmless Chanukah song, said some Hebrew words, lighted some candles, exchanged some presents – a ceremony lasting about ten minutes – and that was all it took to make them the enemy. It did not even take that much. It took nothing" (144).

To her horror, Amy/Anne realizes that the power of her book would be lost if she were to be discovered alive. With a keen sense of the public role that her legacy now plays, she recognizes why the diary must be seen as the work of a ghost: "'They wept for me,' said Amy; 'they pitied me; they prayed for me; they begged my forgiveness. I was the incarnation of the millions of unlived years robbed from the murdered Jews. It was too late to be alive now. I was a saint'" (150). She also gives up her initially optimistic idea of the diary's "mission" (142). Roth portrays the author of the most sentimentalized and apparently uplifting work of Holocaust literature as denying any possibility that her book can change the world. Of her readers, Amy/Anne wonders:

Would suffering come to mean something new to them? Could she actually make them humane creatures for any longer than the few hours it would take to read her diary through? …

What would happen when people had finally seen? The only realistic answer was Nothing. To believe anything else was to yield to longings which even she, the great longer, had a right to question by now. (146)

Roth's Anne rejects any urge toward transcendence, toward a search for meaning in the deaths of the Jews of Europe. She rejects as well the move toward making the Nazis' victims sacred, using the dead for theological affirmation. The only imperative that she can offer is commemoration, her responsibility "to all the slaughtered ... to restore in print their status as flesh and blood ... for all the good that would do them" (147). In this way, Roth, I assume, would not accept the praise of critics who see in the imagined survival of Anne Frank an optimistic turn, "a kind of triumph over history" (Wilson 46). There is in such praise an evasion of the true texture of the novel, of its melancholy tone and its sense of being haunted by presences that are irredeemably lost, dead, unavailable for any triumphant concluding chapter.

The Ghost Writer, in its affirmation of memory and mourning, bears some similarities to the bitter-sweet endings of Bellow's *Mr. Sammler's Planet* and *The Bellarosa Connection*, where the traditional Kaddish prayer is invoked in commemoration of the dead and, as well, to point toward a relationship with the memory of the dead that will in some way reinvigorate the living. Roth, however, ties the imperative of commemoration to literary responsibility, to the commitment made by Amy / Anne and in turn by Nathan to regard their culture with intense and absolutely honest scrutiny. Nathan recognizes that "Higher Education," the story that upset his father, portrays Jews in a less-than-flattering light, but he also believes that through his recollection and inscription of the Newark of his childhood, he is "administering a bear hug" (94). He makes us feel the paradox of the Jewish writer excommunicated by his community in return for the essentially loving care with which he observes and represents it. "Femme Fatale" is such a case of careful regard – an effort to distil from the death of the Franks a usable core of identity for young American Jews and especially for Jewish writers in America. In his attempt to return to Anne her true voice, to mark her experience as particularly Jewish, Nathan risks the accusation that he has written "a desecration even more vile than the one they had read" and despised (171).

With Amy / Anne, Roth devises a mediating figure to overcome the distance (and difference) between his own experience and that of the victims of the Holocaust. In his nuanced portrayal of Anne Frank as a young writer at odds with the contradictory claims of community and commitment to her art, she appears not so much as a projection of Nathan's sexual desire, but as a kind of secret sharer capable of understanding his divided loyalties. Within the fantasy of "Femme Fatale" he is no longer the disinherited artist shouting, "I am on my own!" He has, in effect, recovered a reciprocal relationship in which his dual commitment to art and family can be sustained. His identification with Anne, his efforts at correcting her legacy, and his creation of a fiction meant to address the difficulties of dealing with the Holocaust are all driven by an unshakeable need to come to terms with where he comes from. His search for meaningful literary affiliation is deeply bound up with his desire to be understood by his family. At breakfast the morning after writing "Femme Fatale," Nathan acknowledges that "my father, my mother, the judge and Mrs. Wapter were never out of my thoughts" (157). From this realization he turns to the perfectly comic possibility of marrying Amy/Anne and thereby being true to the expectations of his parents while maintaining his artistic integrity.

This fantasy, ironic and comic at once, is a kind of bitter-sweet joke. Whatever solutions Nathan may discover for his moral, personal, and writerly problems, he accepts that there are no simple ways to address them. There is in his outlook no urge toward a redemptive end nor any overarching moral lesson by which history can be made more bearable. But there is a deep belief in the value of an honest and powerfully imaginative account of these dilemmas, and in the possibility of putting to significant use the narrative legacy of the Holocaust. By foregrounding Nathan's (and his own) response to this legacy, Roth's very writerly novel reveals how narrative can be seen to be a "collaborative production of textual meaning" (Greenblatt, *Representing* xi). *The Ghost Writer* traces the varied responses to Anne Frank's text and focuses our attention on the power of literature to interpret and shape our sense of historical events.

6 Ghost Writing: Chava Rosenfarb's *The Tree of Life*

In many ways, Holocaust writing – fiction, memoirs, and poetry – is about ghosts. The Yizkor Bicher, or memorial books, that appeared after the war gathered survivors' accounts of their lost homes; of the town drunk, the local rabbi, the traders, and the craftspeople who had all been swallowed by the whirlwind. In the work of Elie Wiesel and others even God has become a ghost, an absence that cannot be accounted for, but still haunts a ruined world. And ghosts haunt contemporary fiction that struggles to come to terms with the events of the war, which are distant and foreign, yet central to the consciousness of Canadian and American Jewish novelists. Philip Roth may be our pre-eminent ghost writer. His novels have nurtured reappearances, fantastic revivifications of murdered men and women who represent for him the world destroyed and the possibilities lost with each year taken from the Nazis' victims. By reimagining Bruno Schulz and Anne Frank, Roth attempts not only to come face to face with their writerly worlds and their terrible deaths, but to reinvest our world with the spirit of their writing, its particularity of voice and outlook.

In "'I Always Wanted You to Admire My Fasting'; or, Looking at Kafka," Roth begins his meditation on Kafka by studying his face, seemingly recognizing himself in the famous features, and though Kafka died fifteen years before the war began, Roth cannot help thinking of him within the context of the Holocaust:

I am looking, as I write of Kafka, at the photograph taken of him at the age of forty (my age) – it is 1924, as sweet and hopeful a year as he may ever have known as a man, and the year of his death. His face is sharp and skeletal, a burrower's face: pronounced cheekbones made even more conspicuous by the absence of sideburns; the ears shaped and angled on his head like angel wings; an intense, creaturely gaze of startled composure – enormous fears, enormous control; a black towel of Levantine hair pulled close around the skull the only sensuous feature; there is a familiar Jewish flare in the bridge of the nose, the nose itself is long and weighted slightly at the tip – the nose of half the Jewish boys who were my friends in high school. Skulls chiseled like this one were shoveled by the thousands from the ovens; had he lived, his would have been among them, along with the skulls of his three younger sisters. (247–8)

Ghosts haunt us, and Roth, along with Cynthia Ozick and David Grossman – who each fashioned fictions based on Schulz – pursue them, writing them into our world as a way of contacting the past. A literary ghost also haunts the massive three-volume work *The Tree of Life*, which Montreal writer Chava Rosenfarb first published in Yiddish in 1972 and then in her own translation into English in 1985.[1] Rosenfarb is one of the last surviving contributors to the rich world of Yiddish literature that thrived in Montreal before and just after the war. A.M. Klein drew inspiration from this community, particularly from the poets J.I. Segal and Melech Ravitch, and was constantly in dialogue with it through his reviews in the *Canadian Jewish Chronicle*.[2] Rosenfarb, like many leading figures among Montreal's Jewish writers, arrived in Canada with the burden of an awful past. Born in Lodz in 1923, she survived the notorious ghetto in that city. She taught primary school during the war years, and like most of the Jews who managed to survive the ghetto, she was deported to Auschwitz in September 1944. After the liberation of the camp she lived in Brussels and then came to Montreal in 1950 ("Rosenfarb"). In addition to *The Tree of Life*, which won the Israeli Lamed Prize for Yiddish literature, she is also the author of a number of volumes of poetry and fiction.

Rosenfarb's dual status as novelist and eyewitness provides us with an unparalleled view of the processes by which history is transformed into art. Offering an intricately detailed narrative of the Nazi machinery of destruction, as well as presenting a testament to the lives and struggles of the ghetto's inhabitants, *The Tree of Life* may hold a unique position among the fictions of the Holocaust written by Americans and Canadians. Though the novel bears certain similarities to memoirs of the Holocaust in which the authorial voice is at the centre of the events being narrated, it takes a different approach. In survivors' memoirs of wartime experience, memory is presented with little embellishment. Primo Levi sets the tone for such works in the preface to his early volume *Survival in Auschwitz* (originally titled *If This Is a Man*), where he states sardonically: "It seems to me unnecessary to add that none of the facts are invented" (6). The historical nature of Levi's writings about Auschwitz is reiterated in *The Drowned and the Saved*, published thirty years after *Survival in Auschwitz*: "As for my personal memories, and the few unpublished anecdotes I have mentioned and will mention, I have diligently examined all of them: time has somewhat faded them, but they are in good consonance with their background" (35).

Rosenfarb's novel also falls outside the category of what James Young has called Holocaust documentary fiction, in which the voice of "an eyewitness authority" is fabricated to invest an account with seriousness and integrity ("Historical" 200–4). William Styron's *Sophie's Choice* and D.M. Thomas's *The White Hotel* are well-known examples of such novelistic dependence on historical research.[3] In *The Tree of Life* Rosenfarb draws on her own experience in the ghetto, trusting that "when memory comes, knowledge comes too, little by little" (Friedlander, *When* 182). As a survivor herself and a witness who is also an imaginative writer, she has an inestimable advantage in confronting the difficult material of the Holocaust.

Approaching *The Tree of Life* is a daunting task: it is over one thousand pages long, beginning with a detailed portrait of Jewish life in Lodz before the war and concluding with an epilogue set in post-war Brussels. The novel's autobiographical elements are unmistakable, but more interesting for my purposes are the similarities between it and the compilation of letters and diaries gathered by Alan Adelson and Robert Lapides in *Łódź Ghetto: Inside a Community under Siege*. The experience of reading *The Tree of Life* alongside this collection of documents is much like that recently described by Hilberg as he worked through survivors' accounts: "these people were speaking in unison about virtually identical experiences: what it was like during the last moments of peace, what happened when the Nazis came, how rapidly the Jewish community was engulfed, how family and friends vanished" ("I Was Not There" 18).

Rosenfarb varies her narrative point of view, depicting life in the ghetto through the eyes of a variety of characters, presenting, as Adelson and Lapides's volume strives to do, a "collective consciousness" of wartime Lodz (Adelson xi). Rachel Eibushitz, a young idealistic schoolteacher, is the character whose experience most closely parallels Rosenfarb's. But the drama of Lodz's destruction is viewed in detail through the experiences of Samuel Zuckerman, whose success as a manufacturer and his interest in local Jewish history mark him as a respected, though secularized, community elder. Contrasted with this privileged point of view is that of the family of Itche Mayer, a poor cabinetmaker living in the Baluty section of Lodz, which is walled in to create the ghetto. Rosenfarb's fiction evokes the same lived reality as the documents left behind by those who perished, but she departs from the documentary record. Her attention to historical events, as well as her shaping of those events, will enable us to characterize the ghost that haunts her response to the Holocaust.

The Tree of Life describes historical figures with a great deal of accuracy alongside characters whom we must assume are either composites drawn from the author's experience or essentially fictional. The two most detailed and verifiable portraits in the novel are of Mordecai Chaim Rumkowski, who was installed by the Germans as "Eldest of the Jews" – head of the Lodz Judenrat – and of Simcha Bunim Berkovitch, a character carefully modelled on the Yiddish poet Simcha Bunim Shayevitsh, whose epic poem of the ghetto, *Lekh-Lekho*, was published posthumously after the war. I will return to this poet's role in the novel, which becomes central to the narrative as Rosenfarb confronts issues of memory and obligation to the dead.

Mordecai Chaim Rumkowski, by far the most famous inhabitant of the Lodz ghetto, plays an important role in Rosenfarb's narrative, but one quite unlike that given him by other writers. For some, he has become a rather persistent ghost, an enigmatic figure symbolizing Jewish collaboration with the Nazis, whose theatrical public persona, as well as the real power that he wielded, marks him as larger than life, a distinct and notorious legendary figure amid the obscure, faceless victims of Nazi violence. Alan Adelson refers to

Rumkowski as "perhaps the most controversial Jew in modern history" (xvi). And like Roth with his photo of Kafka, writers have been fascinated by the image of this man, with his shock of white hair, spectacles, and fastidious dress. Primo Levi includes a short rumination on Rumkowski in *The Drowned and the Saved*, in which he attempts to understand the type of personality who could, while proclaiming the need to preserve Jewish life, entertain a certain admiration for the style of government favoured by the Nazis and Italian Fascists. He writes that Rumkowski "had adopted the oratorical technique of Mussolini and Hitler, a style of inspired recitation, the pseudo-colloquy with the crowd, the creation of consent through subjugation and plaudit" (63).

Ample evidence of this identification with the oppressor and mimicry of him can be found in Rumkowski's own words, in the speeches that he gave at ghetto workshops and concerts and in the ghetto's main square. He was not above blaming what he called the ghetto's "parasites" for undermining the community's social fabric (Adelson 201), and in his insistent refrain that Jews would be saved by work there is an unpleasant echo of the cynical slogan *Arbeit Macht Frei*, infamously displayed above the gates of Auschwitz. Rumkowski also took a Führer-like pride in his administrative achievements: "Overnight I erected factories and created a working town. My *Beirat* [council] only knows how to talk. I have carried out my tasks alone, by force. Dictatorship is not a dirty word" (Adelson 146).

In his typically dispassionate fashion, Levi argues that we must suspend judgment on the question of Rumkowski's culpability. He points to the grotesquerie of Rumkowski's rule – his "carriage drawn by a skeleton nag" – and the "astonishing tangle of megalomaniac dream, barbaric vitality, and real diplomatic" skill that supported it (*Drowned* 62–3). For him Rumkowski's behaviour cannot be separated from the general context of human failings in extreme situations, as "we too are so dazzled by power and prestige as to forget our essential fragility" (69).

Saul Bellow, in his novel *Mr. Sammler's Planet*, is less forgiving of Rumkowski, but his approach is similar to Levi's. Sammler often reflects on the "theatricality" for which a personality reaches when challenged by deep feelings of inconsequentiality and fear (235).[4] He sees Rumkowski's predicament as emblematic of the modern condition, of "the weakness of the outer forms which are at present available for our humanity, and the pitiable lack of confidence in them" (236). Bellow presents Rumkowski's actions as the gravest kind of response to this poverty of social and spiritual strength. In reaction to his impotence, Rumkowski fashioned himself as a "King of rags and shit ... ruler of corpses" (236). Both Bellow and Levi are drawn to the case of the "ruler" of the Lodz ghetto for what it can teach us about the modern psyche, first of all, in the extreme deprivations of ghetto existence and, secondly, about the cultural conditions of contemporary life. In *The Tree of Life* we first meet Rumkowski in his pre-war role as the director of an orphanage, abrasively demanding charity from the rich industrialists who run the Lodz Jewish community (20–4). Adelson and Lapides's *Łódź Ghetto* includes sarcastic comments by Jakub Szulman on Rumkowski's success at running a philanthropic institution:

The orphanage flourished and moved to larger quarters in Helenowek, a small village outside of Lodz. And here Rumkowski began experimenting. He introduced a farm, where the children were given instruction in agriculture. He built an orangery. He didn't rest for a minute ... and he won for himself a reputation as a professional *schnorrer*, who had *schnorred* 300,000 zlotys but wouldn't let go of even 30 zlotys. Nothing was unattainable for him. Nothing could stop him. He knew everything, and he could do everything. He was an agronomist, an editor, a pedagogue – all in one. (85)

Once installed by the Germans as the "Eldest of the Jews," Rumkowski began to enjoy his authority, which contributed considerably to his notoriety. Leon Hurwitz records in his diary a remark made by Rumkowski to an associate: "What do you know about power? Power is sweet, power is everything, is life ... But woe to him who makes the slightest attempt to wrest power from me" (Adelson 94). In a scene portraying a visit by Rumkowski to ss Brigadeführer von Strafer's office, Rosenfarb presents Rumkowski's character with a touch of ambiguity:

The Police Chief, Herr von Strafer himself, sat in a broad leather-covered armchair in front of a huge glass-topped desk. On the wall above his head hung a large portrait of the Führer in one of his favourite poses: one hand between the buttons of his green uniform, à la Napoleon ... He had never seen Hitler from so close and with such clarity, and at this very moment he had to admit to his own satisfaction that he, Mordecai Chaim Rumkowski, was firstly, taller than the Führer, and secondly, a handsomer man. (250)

Rumkowski's legendary vanity and fascination with power are tinged with irony here, as Rosenfarb notes that his affinity with German authoritarianism did not include a slavish admiration of the oppressor. Later, when she presents Rumkowski alone, she ascribes to him a degree of self-hatred as well as disdain for his "subjects" that also complicates his identification with his German masters: "Honestly, sometimes I am disgusted with that whole lot of Jewry, with their reproaches, their behaviour, with their wild manners, their lies and falsehoods and with their market-place clamour. Sometimes I'm simply ashamed of being a Jew, I'm disgusted with my own self" (472). This complexity is augmented by the fact that Rosenfarb presents Rumkowski as sincere in his belief that he was a latter-day Moses, a leader of "majestic dignity" (301) ready to "do anything in his power" to protect his people: "He saw himself not in a droshky, but on the hands of the crowds. On their hands they would carry him out of the ghetto and millions of Jews from all corners of the world would join them. They would carry him to Eretz Israel, put the reins of a Jewish homeland into his hands and beg him, 'Be our coachman! Here, lead us! Reign over us, because you are blessed by God, anointed by Him to be a leader, a father, a King of Jews!'" (331).

Rumkowski's personality appeared at its most grotesque in his dealings with subordinates. Jakub Poznanski's diary records that the year "1940 in the ghetto was filled with feverish organizational work: the Chairman running around like crazy, screaming, slapping people's faces, throwing them out [of his office]" (Adelson 41). Rosenfarb echoes this state of affairs when she refers to Rumkowski's warning "that anyone who came to bother him … would get slapped in the face" (499). His bullying of his "subjects" is emulated by Samuel Zuckerman, who manages one of the ghetto factories, but it is worth noting that Rosenfarb is not content to record such perverse antics and goes on to interpret them as the result of the forced breakdown of normal human and communal feeling brought about in the ghetto: "Slapping someone on the face had become for him, as for [Rumkowski], a kind of conditioned reflex. As soon as he noticed such a *klepsydra*[5] face with ashen fallen cheeks, with water bags under the eyes, his hand began to itch. He could not bear the resemblance these unfortunates bore to death masks, and he had to push the sight of such a face away from him, to erase it. This he could accomplish only with a slap" (495).

Rosenfarb relies heavily on her experience and memory, manipulating her narrative to add interpretive or emotional depth. Rumkowski's notorious speech in the autumn of 1942, in which he relayed the Germans' order for the deportation of children, is recorded in the diary of Jozef Zelkowicz, an historian and ethnographer who was on the staff of the ghetto archives and contributed to the unfinished "Encyclopedia of the Ghetto" (Adelson 507).[6] Under the heading "Give Me Your Children," he quotes Rumkowski's words:

A grievous blow has struck the ghetto. They are asking us to give up the best we possess – the children and the elderly ... In my old age I must stretch out my hands and beg: Brothers and sisters, hand them over to me! Fathers and mothers, give me your children! [*Transcriber's note* – Horrifying, terrifying wailing among the assembled crowd.][7] ...

Yesterday afternoon, they gave me the order to send more than 20,000 Jews out of the ghetto, and if not – "We will do it!" So, the question became: "Should we take it upon ourselves, do it ourselves, or leave it for others to do?" Well, we – that is, I and my closest associates – thought first not about "How many will perish?" but "How many is it possible to save?" And we reached the conclusion that, however hard it would be for us, we should take the implementation of this order into our own hands.

I must perform this bloody operation – I must cut off limbs in order to save the body itself! – I must take children because, if not, others may be taken as well, God forbid. [Horrible wailing] (Adelson 328–9)

Rosenfarb compresses this speech, but preserves its morbid flavour, especially Rumkowski's curious combination of pleading and command, of self-dramatization and empathy with the suffering of others:

"Mothers, you must give up your children!" ...
"Mothers!" [Rumkowski] called. "Save the ghetto! If we don't give up the children, not one of us will survive. We shall be erased from the face

of the earth. If life continues, you will have other children. I cannot help it, brothers! They are demanding children up to ten years of age and old people over sixty-five. I took it upon myself to execute the 'action.' If the Germans come in, there will be a blood bath. Mothers! Make this sacrifice for the people! Let everything move smoothly tomorrow ... so that we will be saved." (828)[8]

Rosenfarb's portrait of the "Eldest of the Jews," accurate as it seems to be, does not set him apart from the inhabitants of the ghetto either as a symbolic figure of corrupt power or as an untethered ego, but rather depicts him as enmeshed in the general business and chaos of life in the ghetto. He is a source of fascination and hatred for her characters, but the effect of her presentation of him is to diminish Rumkowski's importance in the imagination as well as in the daily life of the ghetto. Though she depicts him as a public figure fatally compromised by his position and his megalomaniacal temperament, she also takes advantage of the novelist's role to give him an inner life and to allude to aspects of his character that have nothing to do with his role as the German's stooge. She portrays him as a "sentimental Polish patriot" who "loved children" (85), who believed, before the war, that he had betrayed his promise, having failed as a factory owner and a community organizer (93, 100).

Even after the Nazis have appointed him *Älteste der Juden*, Rumkowski is burdened by feelings of inconsequentiality and an "unbearable loneliness" (299). Power for a time does invigorate him; a woman who was raised in his orphanage muses in his presence: "Before her sat a totally different man, proud, imposing" (531). But as the deportations continue and his inability to effect them becomes more obvious, Rosenfarb's Rumkowski does not become more of a despot, but retreats instead into indecision and a habit of delegating the most difficult orders to others (680). Such details contradict the "legend" of Rumkowski, King of the Jews, seized on by writers such as Levi and Bellow and support the ironic comment made by one of Rosenfarb's characters as he appraises the first year of German occupation: "And who could have imagined that Mr. Rumkowski, the bore with the coiffure of a prophet would become the head of the Jewry of Lodz, the *Älteste der Juden*?" (200).

Rumkowski is portrayed in *The Tree of Life* as neither triumphantly aloof and despotic nor courageously sympathetic to the people whom he leads. Like the other ghetto inhabitants, he succumbs to terror, to self-justification, and to sheer bafflement before the Nazis' orders, and ultimately he is robbed of his vitality and his sense of hope. When the Nazis do not need him any longer, he is ordered aboard a freight car without any fanfare, like the hundreds of thousands who preceded him: "The Old Man chewed on his flabby lips and shook his head lower and lower, more and more humbly. But after a while, he slowly began to draw himself up. He wiped his gray mop of hair with his hand, almost knocking his glasses off his nose. He adjusted them, took his wife Clara by the hand and along with her, and his brother Joseph and his sister-in-law Helena, approached the plank leading to the wagon" (1064).

Chaim Rumkowski, presented realistically in his human complexity and ambiguity, does not dominate *The Tree of Life*. Especially in its Yiddish version, the novel is haunted above all by the memory of a much less famous personality, that of Simcha Bunim Shayevitsh, a poet who contributed to the literary life of the ghetto and died at Auschwitz in 1944 (Liptzin 429). Rosenfarb changes his family name to Berkovitch, but otherwise her account of his life and work is historically accurate. Most notably, her description of a long poem that Berkovitch composes over the course of the narrative clearly refers to Shayevitsh's most important work, *Lekh-Lekho*, which was published in 1946 in its original Yiddish by the Lodz Jewish Historical Commission and appears in translation in Adelson and Lapides's *Łódź Ghetto*. The work was inspired by the poet's daughter Blimele, whose imminent transport to Auschwitz motivated Shayevitsh to mine family reminiscences and literary, historical, and biblical allusion in search of peace in the midst of suffering. Rosenfarb's poet also writes poetry to a daughter named Blimele and is at work on a "great poem about the ghetto ... a saga" which is influenced by, among other things, the Torah portion "Lekh-Lekho" (475, 713).[9]

Unlike Rumkowski, Shayevitsh remains an obscure historical figure. He did not leave a literary legacy with the emblematic power of Bruno Schulz's stories or Anne Frank's diary. As with most of the Yiddish writers of his era, the language that had been so natural to him before the war was robbed of its audience by the destruction of most of the world's Yiddish-speaking community. By contrast, the imaginative worlds of Schulz, Anne Frank, and even Rumkowski have become legendary, their lives mythicized, revised, and ruminated upon, though their actual personalities have been obscured by fictional alter egos. Roth goes to some length to counteract the tendency to subsume the actual Anne Frank in a mythical persona in *The Ghost Writer*, and Rosenfarb does the same with Rumkowski. But there is also an important disparity between Roth's treatment of Frank and Rosenfarb's fictional portrait of Shayevitsh. The dead poet is not a figure of desire about whom the narrator of *The Tree of Life* fantasizes; his reappearance as a ghostly presence is harrowing, and Rosenfarb's ghost, unlike Roth's, is not conjured as part of a writerly project – it *comes calling.*

It is in the presentation of the poet Berkovitch that the Yiddish and English versions of *The Tree of Life* differ most markedly. His experience in both is one point from which we view the "collected consciousness" of the ghetto; as the narrative progresses, so does his poem, even as he is gradually robbed of his family, his well-being, and eventually his life. But in the Yiddish original, *Der Boim fun Lebn*, Rosenfarb includes a prologue, set in post-war Brussels, in which Rachel Eibushitz is burdened by her recent past in the ghetto and Auschwitz and by deep feelings of isolation and weariness.[10] As she stands by the window of her Brussels apartment looking at a cherry tree in the nearby rail yard, she is reminded of a tree in the ghetto that was known as "the tree of life." The face of the conductor on a passing train calls to mind a "friend, a poet, who lived in the ghetto." Rachel believes that it is the poet's apparition that "greets her from afar" on this Brussels afternoon, and the voice of the dead man appeals to her so clearly that she begins to argue with it (*Boim* 12–13). This ghostly voice is for her the voice of the past, insisting that she bears a responsibility to collective memory and to the memory of her loved ones.

At first Rachel shrinks from this appeal, fearing that the past can never be overcome but will remain a phantom pleading for attention, an unlovable voice demanding the deepest commitment. "You have come again," is her first response. "Again and again I'll come," the voice answers, asking the question that so many survivors ask of themselves: "Why did you survive? In what way are you better?" (13) Rachel responds, "Maybe I am worse." Yet in the ghostly voice she hears, not recrimination, but solicitation, a call to action that will avert her disquieting "ghetto mood," the "trips to the past" that make her life as a survivor so unsettled (12–14). The ghost demands that Rachel produce a testament to the lives that were lost. Her urge to efface her ghetto mood by forgetting the past is characterized as an act of abandonment. "How can you look at the sun? How can you feel the spring?" the voice asks. "How can you breathe – without me ... without us?" (13).

As this debate proceeds, it becomes clear that the ghost would have Rachel understand that a life without memory can provide only an "unfortunate joy, that flutters like a pale butterfly" around the heart (14). She is assured that she will overcome her fear and weariness through the creative struggle to record her memories: a bond will arise from this difficult memory work, and she will be made whole, more true to herself through her efforts. In Yiddish that does not translate easily into English, the voice urges: "You will feel again your father's hand on your head ... You will encounter again your dearest ones and take unto your life their devotion – their blessing" (16).

The notion of a creative connection with the dead that will invigorate the living is affirmed, as we have seen, in the work of Mandel, Roth, and Richler. We hear as well in this ghostly debate a response to the suffering of others that bears a clear similarity to the philosophy of Emmanuel Levinas, who has written that suffering itself is "useless," as it overwhelms one's humanity "violently and cruelly ... 'for nothing'" ("Useless" 157–8). He adds, however, that awareness of another's suffering raises a "fundamental ethical" challenge, which is "the medication which is my duty. Is not the evil of suffering – extreme passivity, impotence, abandonment and solitude – also ... the possibility of a half opening, and, more precisely, the possibility that wherever a moan, a cry, a groan or a sigh happen there is the original call for aid, for curative help, from the other ego whose alterity, whose exteriority promises salvation?" (158).

Levinas notes how radically this ethical bond was abrogated by the perpetrators of atrocity: "the Holocaust of the Jewish people under the reign of Hitler seems to us the paradigm of gratuitous human suffering" (162). For us, at a remove from the events, there is in this appraisal a call for a "just suffering" in response to the "useless suffering" of the Jews of Europe: "It is this attention to the Other which, across the cruelties of our century – despite these cruelties, because of these cruelties – can be affirmed as the very bond of human subjectivity, even to the point of being raised to a supreme ethical principle – the only one which it is not possible to contest – a principle which can go so far as to command the hopes and practical discipline of vast human groups" (159).

Although Rachel herself has suffered greatly, she was saved from death at the hands of the Nazis. The ghost of the dead poet of Lodz calls on her to attend to the suffering of those who did die, so as to retain a closeness, a kind of contact with them, reaffirming an "inter-human perspective" that Levinas defines as a "non-indifference of one to another ... a responsibility of one for another" (164–5). For Rosenfarb, as for Roth, this responsibility exists even when the object of "non-indifference" is lost, the victim of murder, and it can be expressed through the preservation of memory in writing.

The English translation of *The Tree of Life*, published thirteen years after the Yiddish original, omits the opening frame set in Brussels after the war. The scene, abbreviated and without the ghostly visitation, is placed instead at the end of the novel, reinvoking in only a few lines Rachel's ever-present ghetto mood: "the train reminded her of the cattle train to Auschwitz, while the conductor brought Bunim Berkovitch to mind. It seemed to her that it was he who greeted her from afar, inviting her to board his train; that his voice was telling her, both tenderly and angrily, that her heart, once again, would lead her – there" (1074). It is not clear to me why Rosenfarb made this omission, but by removing the ghostly debate she lessened the sense of urgency with which her novel treats the Holocaust and the commitment to writing about it. Since the English version is already over one thousand pages long without it, its inclusion could not have been seen to extend the novel to an unreasonable length. It may be, however, that with an added thirteen years between her and the war, Rosenfarb no longer felt haunted by the voice of the murdered poet; perhaps she even felt that she could not do justice in English to the intimacy and directness of the original dialogue between Rachel and her ghostly visitor. For Rosenfarb there may well be no language, no viable contemporary form, with which to express her deepest feelings about the Holocaust.

But her exclusion of this section may also point to one of the strategies common in writing by survivors. Susan Suleiman, in an article on autobiographical writing about the war, argues that a certain "narrative withholding" can be found, an unwillingness among authors to reveal themselves completely, based on the fear of being misunderstood: "No one will ever experience my life as I

have, no one will fully understand my story. Will I ever fully understand my story?" (59). Suleiman argues that the writer may find
him or herself "in the position of a reader confronted with a text he
does not understand – a text that, for precisely that reason, he must
continue to read and to write over and over" (48). In this context,
the translation of *Der Boim fun Lebn* can be seen as an independent
work, a retelling of a story "that tries to recover, through writing,
an irrecoverable absence" (Suleiman 60), but does so differently
than its Yiddish original. Why the ghost was written out of *The Tree
of Life* remains a mystery.

PART THREE

Confronting Apocalypse

Forethought:
On Refusing to End

There may be little to be said about Ezra Pound's hatred of the Talmud. Prejudice against things that one does not understand is a tendency that crosses all boundaries. But there may have been a certain method to his madness. With only the barest knowledge of the rabbi's way of thinking, of the roving, self-glossing, ever-ambivalent form of interpretation applied to biblical story and practical legal matters, Pound may have sensed the prospect of an *interminable* discussion, a manner of formulating meaning by way of a community of varying responses that is the very antipode to the intellectual atmosphere he found in Mussolini's Italy. Michael André Bernstein points out that for both the fascist and the communist, history was "monologic" and "monolithic." The "impulse toward individual choices, with its attendant debates and uncertainties was regarded as the Jewish ('talmudic') vice *par excellence*" (37). This manner of thought – though by no means practised or necessarily understood by contemporary writers – has left its mark on the modern Jewish imagination. Its legacy is a mistrust of final judgments and apocalyptic scenes of closure. Instead, Jewish writers often counter apocalyptic narratives by presenting novelistic worlds that do not resolve, but are made up of "a mosaic of conscious and unconscious citation of earlier discourse" (Boyarin, *Intertexuality* 12). This strategy develops a dialogue with authority and tradition. Such hybridized fictions – those that mix genres, as well as contemporary with historical concerns – lead a literary work to enter an already existing dialogue, rather than present any final scenes of instruction.

7 Apocalypse Stalled: The Role of Traditional Archetype and Symbol in Nathanael West's *Miss Lonelyhearts* and *The Day of the Locust*

Much of the criticism dealing with Nathanael West's two slim novels, *Miss Lonelyhearts* and *The Day of the Locust*, has been devoted to a reading of their apocalyptic temper. It is worth noting that West's stature as a writer in the apocalyptic vein has been most strenuously proclaimed since the mid-sixties, when the entire tradition of American fiction fell under the scrutiny of commentators hunting for archetypes of cataclysm and spiritual degeneration.[1] In an influential essay entitled "Days of Wrath and Laughter" first published in 1965, R.W.B. Lewis proclaimed that America was in "a resoundingly apocalyptic mood" (184) and that the work of Nathanael West provided the finest example of this "thickening American chaos" (212). Robert Alter in "The Apocalyptic Temper" took issue with Lewis's insistence on the profundity of America's apocalyptic tendencies, but not without admitting that *The Day of the Locust* was informed by the "schematic imagination" of "apocalyptic assumptions" (63). His polemical response to Lewis's essay denounced the apocalyptic vein as an undesirable direction for American fiction, arguing that the apocalyptic imagination tended "to go skittering off into the upper reaches of the cosmos ... to view humanity abstractly, as swarms of odious insects, beetles, or locusts" (65).

Alter is less kind to West than is Lewis, intimating that the novelist's "apocalyptic assumptions" tended to limit, rather than extend, his fiction (63). Interestingly enough, a writer who knew

West well and who played an important role in getting his work published did not even mention these weighty concerns in his early efforts at puffing *Miss Lonelyhearts*. William Carlos Williams, touting West to an Italian readership as "A New American Writer," pointed instead to his friend's treatment of contemporary historical and social issues, as he reviewed *Miss Lonelyhearts* in 1933 (Martin 153). He saw the novel as an accurate depiction of the "moral impoverishment of our youth in the cities" and an expression of "what scoundrels we've become in this century" (qtd. in Martin 153–4). And true to his own personal literary agenda, Williams characterized West as a writer who was developing a true American voice, a "dialect natural to [our] condition" (qtd. in Martin 153). Between the specifically American and contemporary nature of Williams's remarks and the more general and mythic readings of critics such as R.W.B. Lewis, we must try to find a ground on which to uncover the true character of West's apocalyptic assumptions, a ground on which we can ask toward what end they are directed.

There is little evidence that West's interest in apocalyptic themes is motivated by a conscious urge to investigate the Jewish literary and cultural history from which they derive. Among the Jewish American novelists who came to the fore in the 1930s and 1940s, West proves one of the most difficult to interpret from the vantage point of his cultural inheritance. Investigations along these lines run aground for lack of evidence and are further scuttled by the flippancy of West's own treatment of the issue. "Horace Greely said, Go west young man, so I did," was his stock response to queries about why he gave up a notably German Jewish name for an American one (Locklin 7). West's biographer offers a detailed portrait of the assimilated surroundings in which West grew up on New York's Upper East Side, where everything, from the family's refusal to speak Yiddish to its discomfort in acknowledging its European past, suggests a studied flight from all things Jewish (Martin 20, 25). This tendency is noted in the young West by a university friend: "more than anyone I ever knew, Pep writhed under the accidental curse of his religion … he never denied that he was a Jew, and so far as I know he never changed his faith … But he changed his name, he changed his clothes, he changed his manners" (Light 144).

It is not, it seems, an urge to link his biblical inheritance with an American identity that motivates West to write his two apocalyptic novels. Instead, as Williams, Alter, and Lewis all suggest, it is his recognition of the suitability of apocalyptic narratives to an investigation of a growing American chaos. Each of these critics, however, addresses this chaos in a widely divergent manner, making use of different points of departure and different theoretical frameworks. Williams's Depression-era remarks are focused on a prevalent moral decay, but the poet makes no claims upon any grander concern than the immediate American condition. He sounds more like an angry sociologist than a prophet, as he insists that the "cities are rotten and desperate" and that such social unrest must be faced by those who are "lying in a bed of roses" (qtd. in Martin 154).

Robert Alter's examination of the representation of disintegrating society in American fiction offers an excellent counterpoint to Williams's purely secular account. He makes no attempt to engage the American scene circa 1966, but concentrates instead on denouncing the apocalyptic pose as an "inhuman" and "spiritually irresponsible" context within which to cast this chaos (62). The undercurrent of Alter's argument is of purely theological import. He characterizes apocalyptic yearnings as having derived from "a decadent form of Judaism," and as having been rejected by Judaism "in favor of competing 'translations' of the vision of man and history articulated by the prophets" (62–3). Alter also takes aim at "apocalypse" as being one of the more familiar "timeless archetypes" that is too commonly used to straitjacket a literary work (61).

R.W.B. Lewis's examination of the "thickening American chaos" takes a middle ground somewhere between the secular appraisal of Williams and the orthodox imperatives of Alter. He discusses at length the biblical origins of apocalypse, outlining its ten key traits as follows:

(1) periodic natural disturbances, earthquakes and the like; (2) the advent and the turbulent reign of the Antichrist ... (3) the second coming of Christ and (4) the resultant cosmic warfare (Armageddon) that brings in (5) the millennium ... (6) the gradual degeneration of human and physical nature, the last and worst apostasy (or falling away from God), featured by (7) the second and briefer "loosening of Satan"; (8) an ultimate catastrophe, the end of the world by fire; (9) the Last Judgment; and (10) the appearance of the new heaven and earth. (196–7)

Lewis's method (like that of many of the authors cited below) derives from an urge to discover elements of the apocalyptic mythos in West's work. His conceptual framework is ultimately literary, and not theological, as is Alter's. "Days of Wrath and Laughter" is explicit about its intention of examining the way in which American writers are using "the conventional machinery of the apocalyptic tradition" (206). Lewis points to a "rebirth" of images in American writing and a "reanimating of those great and ancient archetypes by which Western man has periodically explained to himself the full range of his condition, and the most spectacular of his expectations or terrors" (206). At no point in his manifesto on the "thickening chaos" in America does he introduce the suggestion of a coming religious rebirth. He is solely concerned with a literary renaissance and an examination of the mythic material that supports it. One is reminded here of the familiar saying which asserts that when a divine world falls and is no longer believed in, its inhabitants are bound to become the figures of poetry. Through a close reading of *Miss Lonelyhearts* and *The Day of the Locust*, I will try to discern whether Nathanael West's apocalyptic assumptions are based on an authentic redemptive eschatology or upon a renaissance of literary archetypes.

THE APOCALYPTIC BACKGROUND

Although the apocalyptic temper has shown itself to be supported by an unusually resilient structure of myth and symbol, the urge to predict the end of days is undoubtedly felt more keenly in some eras than in others. R.W.B. Lewis links the contemporary American idea of apocalypse with sixteenth-century notions of revelation and imminent catastrophe (198). This late season of the medieval age "was marked by violence and a new and pervasive pessimism," and the dissolution of the medieval world view led to dramatic breaks with established cultural structures: "the Church was straining and cracking under the onslaught of the growth of cities, the new vigor of commerce and capitalism, the rise of national states, the demands for religious reform and the beginnings of science" (Meisler 42–3). The best-known artistic expressions of this era's premonitions of doom may well be the ominous grotesqueries of Hieronymus Bosch and Pieter Bruegel the Elder. The popular appeal and subsequent decline of interest in their works offers us an instructive example of the unpredictable rise and fall of apocalyptic fears. Bosch was widely admired as one of the "most perceptive, most apocalyptic masters" of his time – public notices of his death described him as a "very famous painter" – but his cryptic work quickly fell out of favour with the wealthy Dutch burghers who had commissioned it, and Bosch's reputation is said to have been on the decline less than a hundred years after his death in 1516 (Meisler 41, 55). By 1621 the painter's visions were far enough out of line with a less pessimistically inclined Europe that his name came to be used as a term of opprobrium. One Spanish poet is reputed to have withered a rival by dismissing his work as "absurd rubbish, you Bosch among the poets, nothing but devils, buttocks and cod-pieces" (Meisler 55).

A similar rise and fall of apocalyptic fervour can be traced in the early years of Puritan settlement in America. Apocalyptic concerns were at the forefront of the new culture's self-image, as it inscribed its experiment in the New World within "the field of the battle between Christ and Satan" (Lewicki 6). Zbigniew Lewicki has argued that the millennial fervour of the first wave of settlers was undermined by the growing secularization of American culture, and he makes the intriguing assertion that this movement toward a secular society throughout the eighteenth and nineteenth centuries brought about a state in which "apocalypse ... virtually disappeared from American fiction of the first half of our century, with the possible exception of Nathanael West" (xvi).

If the rise of secularism did suppress the apocalyptic strain in the American imagination, a concern with cultural disintegration and cataclysm was forced back to the forefront of literary and historical studies in the wake of the Holocaust. This event marks another breakdown of established order at least as momentous as the waning of the Middle Ages, and has led to the re-examination of such traditional paradigms as apocalypse, in an attempt to discover if such patterns of myth and symbol might in part have motivated and given substance to the Nazi world-view. In an important essay on post-Holocaust culture, George Steiner lifts the apocalyptic vision out of its traditional religious or mythic context and recontextualizes it in terms of deep psychological motives:

It is precisely from the 1830s onward that one can observe the emergence of a characteristic "counter-dream" – the vision of the city laid waste, the fantasies of Scythian and Vandal invasion, the Mongol steeds slaking their thirst in the fountains of the Tuileries gardens. An odd school of painting develops: pictures of London, Paris or Berlin seen as colossal ruins, famous landmarks burnt, eviscerated or located in a weird emptiness among charred stumps and dead water ... Exactly a hundred years later these apocalyptic collages and imaginary drawings of the end of Pompeii, were to be our photographs of Warsaw and Dresden. It needs no psychoanalysis to suggest how strong a part of wish-fulfillment there was in these nineteenth-century intimations. (23–4)

Steiner characterizes these "apocalyptic collages" as western European culture's projection of its own ennui and emptiness, and as the imagined end of an era for which traditional paradigms of faith and order had failed. The distinctly unredemptive vision of Vandals gloating over Europe's decimated cities is not in *spirit* an apocalyptic vision, but somehow so only in form. Such paintings might be said to deploy "scattered remnants of the apocalyptic vocabulary" for their own creative purposes (Lewis 206).

THE NOVELIST'S TABLEAU

In *The Day of the Locust*, Nathanael West meditates on a school of painting much like that described by George Steiner. Tod Hackett, the novel's painter-cum-set-designer, finds himself trapped within the maze of cast-off sets that litter a Hollywood back lot, and he recognizes, among the detritus of abandoned masonry, a scene reminiscent of the seventeenth-century painter Salvator Rosa: "There were partially demolished buildings and broken monuments, half hidden by great, tortured trees, whose exposed roots writhed dramatically in the arid ground, and by shrubs that carried, not flowers or berries, but armories of spikes, hooks and swords" (West, *Day* 132).[2] The final flourish of this passage – the infernal shrubs bearing arms – reminds us not only of Rosa's depiction of ruins surrounded by dramatic Italian landscape, but also of the complicated visions of Bosch and Bruegel. We find West entering here, by way of this symbolism, into the realm of the grotesque, a world in which "a frightful mixture of mechanical, vegetable, animal and human elements is represented as the image of our world, which is breaking apart" (Kayser 33).

West's fiction is rich in this kind of symbolism, wherein natural objects – commonly suggestive of ripeness, unfurling vision, even revelation – operate in ways completely inimical to their usual identity. In *Miss Lonelyhearts* a driving tour takes Miss Lonelyhearts by New Haven, a place whose name is suggestive of a transcendent beginning in the wilderness, and beneath trees whose leaves are "shaped and colored like candle flames" (36). But as the initial transformative character of the trip is shattered, the leaves no longer burn skyward like souls ascending, but hang "straight down" and shine in the hot sun "like an army of little metal shields" (38). Wolfgang Kayser has pointed to the possible link between such grotesque symbolism of admixture (leaves as shields, flowers as swords) and the language of biblical apocalypse. He refers to the famous passage in the Book of Revelation in which locusts with the faces of men, bearing iron breastplates, are seen to rise from the smoke of a gaping abyss (9:7–11). The more markedly apocalyptic books of the Hebrew Bible and the Apocrypha offer similar instances of such grotesque visions of our everyday world breaking apart. One of Daniel's visions includes a man with a body like beryl and arms and legs of bronze (10:6). And in a late apocalyptic book, 2 Esdras, the end of days includes a transmogrification of the known world in which "Blood shall drip from wood, / and the stone shall utter its voice" (5:5).

It is agreed among almost all commentators on biblical apocalypse that such enigmatic portents predict the arrival of a transcendental reality (Collins, "Towards" 9). Jacques Derrida writes that "we know that every apocalyptic eschatology is promised in the name of light, of seeing and vision, and of a light of light, of a light brighter than all the lights it makes possible" ("Of an Apocalyptic" 82).

Although West's writing is replete with the symbolism of grotesque admixture, which is often used to signify a world breaking apart, he does not make use of this symbolism to promise any light of lights. And it is at this point that a more thorough morphology of the apocalyptic genre must be developed to bring us toward a deeper discussion of his symbolism and its attendant world-view.

Martin Buber has characterized the apocalyptic tradition by outlining its differences from prophecy. The task of the prophet, according to Buber, was not to predict but to "confront man with alternatives of decision" (177). The prophetic voice acted as an exhortation to dialogue, a call to action which insisted that "the future is not fixed, for God wants men to come to him with full freedom" (Buber 178). The apocalyptic voice, which appeared as the prophetic tradition withered, intimates that humankind has nothing left to achieve and is helpless under the sway of a kind of historical determinism:

The mature apocalyptic, moreover, no longer knows a historical future in the real sense. The end of all history is near. Creation has grown old.

[There is] no longer room for an alternative: the future is spoken of as being established from the beginning. (Buber 183, 178)

Robert Alter restates Buber's argument in even more emphatic terms: "In the prophets, God works through men in history, with the promise of bringing history to a fulfillment; in Jesus's teaching, God stands posed to lop off history, suddenly, in the night" (64).

The rise of apocalypticism, then, is inextricably bound up with a sense of helplessness, of threat; and the attitude which must support this outlook is often developed among a subject people who feel themselves to be "laboring under a strong sense of persecution" (McGinn 526). This self-perception is what underlies the apocalyptic's urge to reveal his visionary message to those who, as outcasts from an oppressive status quo, will be drawn to an alternative code. Since the apocalyptic writer is bent on revealing "mysteries beyond the bounds of normal knowledge" to a select group of "worthies," he is often drawn to enigmatic symbols, covert codes, and the passing of secrets through cryptic language ("Apocalypse"). We are reminded here of Bosch's bizarre visionary system of symbols and the nearly untranslatable iconography of the Book of Revelation. In the latter, even after a vision of the end of things is offered to the book's writer, a "voice from heaven" insists that the vision's recipient "seal up those things which the seven thunders uttered and write them not" (10:4). Precedent for this exhortation to secrecy is found in the Book of Daniel, where the matters revealed remain unintelligible to their recipient and are to be hidden in sealed books until the time of their full revelation comes to pass (12:4, 9). In the late apocalyptic book 2 Esdras this formula is repeated in its entirety, as its author is told to protect "this secret of the most high" and to "write all these things that you have seen in a book, and put it in a hidden place" (12:37).

Jacques Derrida, in an article devoted to the apocalyptic tone in recent philosophy, characterizes the conveyor of apocalyptic texts as a "mystagogue" who "takes you aside, speaks to you in a private code, and whispers secrets to you in uncovering your ear for you, jumbling, covering, or parasitizing the voice of reason" (72). The mystagogue, then, denies a given way of "knowing" the world – he or she upends the rational with the mysterious. West provides a stinging parody of this figure, in its American incarnation, in *The Day of the Locust*:

One Friday night in the "Tabernacle of the Third Coming," a man near Tod stood up to speak. Although his name most likely was Thompson or Johnson and his home town Sioux City, he had the same countersunk eyes, like the heads of burnished spikes, that a monk by Magnasco might have. He was probably just in from one of the colonies in the desert near Soboda Hot Springs where he had been conning over his soul on a diet of raw fruit and nuts. He was very angry. The message he had brought to the city was one that an illiterate anchorite might have given decadent Rome. It was a crazy jumble of dietary rules, economics and Biblical threats. He claimed to have seen the Tiger of Wrath stalking the walls of the citadel and the Jackal of Lust skulking in the shrubbery, and he connected these omens with "thirty dollars every Thursday" and meat eating. (142)

This imagery echoes one of Shrike's lectures, in which he mocks Miss Lonelyhearts's ambition to become a religious visionary. Writing a "letter to Christ" in his friend's name, Shrike satirizes the mystagogic tone: "I am twenty-six years old and in the newspaper game. Life for me is a desert of empty comfort ... The Leopard of Discontent walks the streets of my city; the Lion of Discouragement crouches outside the walls of my citadel. All is desolation and a vexation of the spirit. I feel like hell" (*Miss* 35). Both of these passages echo, and parody, Jeremiah's prophecy of Israel's destruction: "Therefore a lion from the forest shall slay them, a wolf from the desert shall destroy them, a leopard is watching against their cities, every one who goes out of them shall be torn in pieces" (5:6).

West's presentation of mystagoguery American-style suggests that it has no authenticity – it mixes its metaphors and obscures any particular vision with a pastiche of unrelated fragments and references. Shrike's parody of a visionary's self-mortification blends biblical language with the hard-boiled slang of detective fiction. The sunken-eyed shouter at the Tabernacle of the Third Coming constructs an unfocused conglomeration of faddist concerns and disconnected biblical references, and conveys a deep interest in the almighty U.S. dollar. In *Miss Lonelyhearts*, West offers an even more perverse sectarian mythology. Shrike carries a clipping in his wallet that describes a man condemned to die for murdering a recluse "over a small amount of money" (7). The murderer will be honoured by a ceremony combining animal sacrifice and the manipulation of figures on an adding machine (7). West's biographer, Jay Martin, points out that there are equal parts of accurate reportage and wild confabulation in these sectarian combinations of seemingly incompatible mythic and symbolic codes. He points out that the leading seller on the American book lists in 1925 and 1926 was a volume written by an adman entitled *The Man Nobody Knows*, which portrayed Jesus "as the first modern business and advertising man, 'the founder of modern business' ... [The author] declared that Christ's parables are brilliant examples of advertising, that he had known and used 'every one of the principles of modern salesmanship,' and that his great triumph was that he had 'picked up twelve men from the bottom ranks of business and forged them into an organization'" (Martin 180).

Whether intentionally or by coincidence, West's parodies of mystagoguery in America make use of a formal feature that is central to all apocalyptic writing. This element is what Derrida has referred to as the "apocryptic, apocryphal, masked, coded" quality of the genre,

its cryptic ruses. By its very tone, the mixing of voices, genres, and codes, and the breakdown [*le détraquement*] of destinations, apocalyptic discourse can also dismantle the dominant contract or concordat ... Conversely, we could even say that every discourse of every tonal disorder, everything that untunes and becomes inadmissable in general collocution, everything that is no longer identifiable starting from established codes, from both sides of one front, will necessarily pass for or be considered mystagogic, obscurantist, and apocalyptic. ("Of an Apocalyptic" 89–90)

It is this formal feature of apocalyptic writing that bears a striking similarity to the language of the grotesque. E.H. Gombrich describes grotesque art as being made up of "elusive dream imagery in which 'all things are mixed' ... It outrages both our 'sense of order' and our search for meaning ... Thus there is nothing to hold on to, nothing fixed, the *deformitas* is hard to 'code' and harder still to remember, for everything is in flux" (qtd. in Harpham, 42). He goes on to say that the grotesque is "linked with the enigmatic, the mysterious" (qtd. in Harpham 42). These formal affinities between the two genres and, more important, the ontological affinities that they suggest account for the equally hostile reception suffered by writing perceived to be either apocalyptic or grotesque. Wolfgang Kayser describes numerous aestheticists' dislike for grotesque images, which have often been accused of inciting an "agonizing fear of the dissolution of our world" (31). Derrida, in his account of Immanuel Kant's dislike for the apocalyptic tone, points to the philosopher's belief that the recourse to enigma and cryptic secrets serves only "to derange, to put out of order, to jumble" the voice of reason ("Of an Apocalyptic" 72). A more antique, but no less fervent, condemnation of apocalyptics is found in the rabbinic text Baraita, which assumes an uncharacteristically nasty tone with regard to Christian and Gnostic apocalypses: "These writings and the books of the heretics are not to be saved from a fire but are to be burnt whenever found" ("Apocalypse").

It may not be unreasonable to argue that in the case of the rabbis, as in that of Kant, we are listening to a normative, conservative voice bent on repressing a visionary text that is seen as a potential threat to the established order. In *Miss Lonelyhearts* it is the cynical voice of mainstream, materialist American culture that represses the visionary gleam. At Delehanty's speakeasy one of the regulars characterizes spiritual desire as a frivolous hobby: "What I say is, after all one has to earn a living. We can't all believe in Christ" (15). During the same conversation, Shrike suggests that the visionary pose is nothing more than an affectation, a kind of decadent poetic style: "Well that's the trouble with his approach to God. It's too damn literary – plain song, Latin poetry, medieval painting, Huysmans, stained-glass windows and crap like that" (14). In his search for an authentic visionary voice, Miss Lonelyhearts finds that his imagination is saturated with the dominant secular discourse. In what appears to be a deep-felt urge to give spiritual succour to the Doyles, he manages "merely [to write] a column for his paper" (49). West's decision to make *The Brothers Karamazov* a touchstone for his would-be devotee leads us to Dostoyevsky's novel for further instances of spiritual desire belittled by a cynical status quo. There is a noteworthy similarity between Miss Lonelyhearts and the monk Father Zossima, whose messianic vision, delivered in a deathbed manifesto on a monk's calling, is denigrated and sneered at by his more cynical colleagues (Dostoyevsky 174–8). Miss Lonelyhearts seems to model his room after Zossima's, with its monastic chair, table, and icon, and West may be recalling the engraving that hangs on the monk's wall when he writes that Miss Lonelyhearts's room is "as full of shadows as an old steel engraving" (8).

Inhibited by the attitudes held by his colleagues, as well as by Betty, who seems to confuse any kind of spiritual malaise with a case of the flu, Miss Lonelyhearts cannot derive anything of value from his mystagogic urge. At the outset of the novel, he gives the impression that he will begin a stereotypic speech declaiming a decrepit society, but the introductory phrase – "Ah, humanity" – gives way to the sense that he is "heavy with shadow" (5). With this phrase, West precludes the possibility of his hero encountering even a spark of revelatory light. The appearance of shadow at this moment of mystagogic utterance is a subtle intimation of what I will call West's anti-apocalyptic imagination: "Shadow in Christian theology is defined as deprivation. Like evil, it is known through absence and not through presence ... The time of shade is not seen against a backdrop of apocalyptic possibility, where time may be stopped and light prevail. It moves downward to darkness" (Cook, "Decreations" 20). In an earlier scene, West intimates that Miss Lonelyhearts himself is to blame for his spiritual blankness, as he courts a kind of meditative ecstasy, and upon nearing its fulfilment, becomes "frightened and close[s] his eyes," choosing darkness over vision (9).

Although Miss Lonelyhearts is portrayed as a stalled spiritualist, West does allow him a number of visionary moments that might well be described as enigmatic or mysterious. Like the biblical mystagogue, he receives some of this visionary material through dreams. One such dreamscape seems to be a conglomeration of motifs common to the surrealist paintings of Giorgio de Chirico and René Magritte: "a train rolled into a station where he was a reclining statue holding a stopped clock, a coach rumbled into the yard of an inn where he was sitting over a guitar, cap in hand, shedding the rain with his hump" (51; see illus. 1). The stopped clock, the statue, and the ubiquitous locomotive are three of the most repeated figures in de Chirico's early paintings of empty plazas. In West these sur-realist juxtapositions make up a cryptic code – the stopped clock presages some kind of doom; the dreamer's dual role as hunchback and statue are intimations of a denatured humanity – but the images do not resonate with any clear message. The enigmatic nature of this scene precludes any kind of resolution.

Here we can make use of an argument put forward by Eleanor Cook, which might help us refine our sense of the relationship between cryptic imagery and apocalyptic texts. She argues, with reference to the poetry of Wallace Stevens, that if an enigma remains too thoroughly (and possibly intentionally) closed, it may prove to be "self-contained and antiapocalyptic ... it does not resolve" (*Poetry* 16). The section of *Miss Lonelyhearts* entitled "Miss Lonelyhearts in the Dismal Swamp" begins with such an irresolvable tableau. Like the dream reminiscent of de Chirico, this scene contains a fairly explicit intimation of a coming cataclysm, as Miss Lonelyhearts muses, "All order is doomed, yet the battle is worth while" (31). But this mystagogic declaration is interrupted when "his imagination beg[ins] again to work" and he envisions a pawn-shop full of junk and pieces of useless tools. Like the sunken-eyed devotee in *The Day of the Locust*, he struggles with a pastiche of symbolic systems that will not combine into any authentic vision. He sorts through not only cast-off clothes but cast-off icons as well, as he experiments with "a circle, triangle, square, swastika. But nothing proved definitive" (31). A "gigantic cross" holds his interest somewhat longer than his previous experiments, but the particular symbol disappears behind the jumble of refuse out of which it is built – "bottles, shells, chunks of cork, fish heads, pieces of net" (31).

This pastiche of uncodable elements is, I would argue, anti-apocalyptic; it is enigmatic in a thoroughly closed and non-revelatory way. Still, Miss Lonelyhearts's hallucinations retain what Kayser has described as the grotesque vision's ability to "portray the inexplicable, incomprehensible, ridiculous" (35). The disorder of the pawn-shop and of the gathering garbage on the strand presents a vision of a culture reverting to chaos. Miss Lonelyhearts's need to organize this mess – an urge he refers to earlier in the novel as "an almost insane sensitiveness to order" (10) – is based on the "agonizing fear" of the dissolution of his world (Kayser 31). West depicts his hero, overcome by this fear, as he flees into a streetscape where the laws that rule our familiar world do not appear to hold: "there chaos was multiple. Broken groups of people hurried past, forming neither stars nor squares. The lamp-posts were badly spaced and the flagging was of different sizes. Nor could he do anything with the harsh clanging sound of street cars and the raw shouts of hucksters. No repeated group of words would fit their rhythm and no scale could give them meaning" (11).

During one of Miss Lonelyhearts's strolls through a neighbour-hood park, he is confronted by a similar sense of the recognizable order being distorted. The Mexican War obelisk that dominates the park becomes tumescent and seems "as though it [is] about to spout a load of granite seed" (19). This transformation of the inanimate into the animate, and its appearance before the would-be mysta-gogue as some kind of sign, leads not to revelation but to flight. And like his earlier urge to declaim humanity's woes, which is overcome by "shadow" (5), this vision casts "a long, rigid shadow … in the dying sun" (19). Moving toward darkness and an indeci-sive message, West's imagery retains its grotesque character. The obelisk is an exemplary figure of a world "in flux" (Gombrich; qtd. in Harpham 42); it represents a vision that includes "the fusion of spheres, the monstrous nature of ingredients, and the subversion of order and proportion" (Kayser 29). But this figure offers no intima-tion of revelatory light. The red sun at dusk and the tumescent tower are more suggestive of chaos and the machinery of torture than of any kind of eschatological salvation. Once again, West's grotesque imagery is not set against a backdrop of apocalyptic possibility, but is suggestive of an ongoing transmutation and dete-rioration of his characters' surroundings.

West's tumescent obelisk points to a blurring of the division between nature and man-made objects, which can be seen in many of the paintings of Hieronymus Bosch. In the triptych entitled *The Garden of Earthly Delights*, promontories over a central lake are made of rock, spriglike outcroppings, and the glass beakers used by alche-mists (illus. 2). In Bosch's St Antony triptych the sky in the central panel is plied by winged objects that are half bird, half battleship. An even more horrible hybrid of man-made and natural elements appears in a work by Pieter Bruegel entitled *The Triumph of Death* (illus. 3). This painting depicts an apocalyptic landscape in which trees have been transformed into a species of gallows or torture machine.

Tod Hackett's work in progress in *The Day of the Locust* – "The Burning of Los Angeles" – has many features in common with this tradition of apocalyptic painting. Like Bosch's panorama of hell in the right panel of *The Garden of Earthly Delights*, it will be topped, "parallel with the frame," by "the burning city" (184). He foresees the canvas showing the "city burning at high noon, so that the flames [will] have to compete with the desert sun and thereby appear less fearful, more like bright flags flying from roofs and windows than a terrible holocaust" (118). This tableau bears an uncanny resemblance to the centre panel of Bosch's St Antony triptych, where a town being swallowed by flames blends, almost inconspicuously, into the upper corner of the image and is flush with a bright daytime horizon. In the foreground of this bizarre juxtaposition, a crowd goes about its business, oblivious to the neighbouring carnage.

Tod's motif of a mob winding down "a long hill" and "spilling into the middle foreground" of a landscape (184) is common to the apocalyptic visions of both Bosch and Bruegel. Both painters use this formal aspect to draw the viewer's eye from a background of conflagration, along a winding mass of humanity, through an area of struggle, to a more or less unbothered panorama of men and women consumed by their everyday business. Bruegel's *Dulle Griet* makes use of crumbling structures and curious ramparts to mark this descending sweep with hidden sites of battle and torture (illus. 4). In the hell panorama of Bosch's *Garden of Earthly Delights*, the mass winds its way down lighted streets to a mid-point in the painting, where it seems to march directly down a ladder into the fires of hell. Tod does not mention Bosch and Bruegel as influences, but he does remark that his painting will not derive from the American tradition. Instead, it will make use of European influences devoted to portraying the horrors of war and humanity's grotesque character: "From the moment he had seen [the Angelenos], he had known that, despite his race, training and heritage, neither Winslow Homer nor Thomas Ryder could be his masters and he turned to Goya and Daumier" (60).

Although Tod is quick to condemn the "disordered minds" that he assumes must propel the visionaries who visit California's crack-pot tabernacles, he does admit to his own mystagogic urge and its effect upon his plans for "The Burning of Los Angeles" (142). His vision is motivated by pure premonition, by an expectation of events that he is not entirely convinced will come true, but which he considers to be somehow determined by fate. At one point his musing over the painting brings him to the conclusion that there will "be civil war," and he counts himself among the "prophets of doom and destruction" (118). Like all good mystagogues, Tod watches his fellows – their ennui and bitter feelings of disaffection – for portents and for "signs of the times that [will] reveal the immanence of the appointed end" (McGinn 526).

Since West has characterized Tod as a painter and a prophet of cataclysm, one might expect him to vouchsafe his Hollywood visionary a taste of the transfiguring, revelatory light that must follow all apocalyptic promises. But *The Day of the Locust* moves not toward revelatory light, but toward darkness; not toward a transfiguring unveiling of a new reality, but to a stubborn refusal of closed figures to open. The hidden leaves remain unread, and the cataclysmic landscape promises no garden of earthly delights.

I take as the signpost of West's irredeemable landscape the ever-present eucalyptus tree that appears on street corners, on back lots, and even on the outskirts of Tod Hackett's Hollywood. As a recurrent symbol it is notably inert, and more than once it serves as a site of covert action – an object behind which to hide. Eleanor Cook tells us that eucalyptus "means 'well covered,' as the flower of the eucalyptus tree is, until its time for uncovering arrives in the ordinary course of things" (*Poetry* 269). Such an ordinary, everyday uncovering – eucalypsis – can be set in opposition to the "sudden, extraordinary uncovering of things" that is commonly referred to as apocalypse (Cook, *Poetry* 269).

Like many of West's symbols, the eucalyptus appears first with intimations of endless possibility, and it hints as well at an uncovering or opening towards vision. Once Tod has moved into the San Bernadino Arms, his room provides him with a view of a "spray of eucalyptus," whose leaves stir in the breeze, showing "first their green side, then their silver one" (62). The Whitmanian pun on leaves may not be altogether irrelevant to West's image here, as Tod's view both promises a display of natural signs and is suggestive of open books – of leaves that must be read. But following this appearance, the eucalyptus leaves of the Hollywood Hills remain resolutely covered or are ignored altogether. In descriptions of the landscape surrounding Homer Simpson's house and of the hills where Earl Shoop and his buddies camp, the eucalyptus tree is mentioned only incidentally (80, 113). On his trek through a movie back lot, Tod conceals himself by a eucalyptus tree, which, considering the nature of its surroundings, may well be ersatz (133).

The eucalyptus makes its final appearance as a landmark at the centre of the mêlée that takes place at the novel's conclusion, in front of Khan's Persian Palace. At the outset of this climactic scene, Adore Loomis uses the tree to hide behind as he tries, unsuccessfully, to catch Homer's attention with a purse tied to a string (180). As this gathering of "screwballs and screwboxes" deteriorates into a tableau of a world spinning out of control (184), the eucalyptus tree proffers the promise of a calm centre, of a landscape marked with recognizable objects. But this site of order and security remains unattainable: "Using the eucalyptus tree as a landmark, [Tod] tried to work toward it by slipping sideways against the tide, pushing hard when carried away from it and riding the current when it moved toward his objective. He was within only a few feet of the tree when a sudden, driving rush carried him far past it" (181).

Inscrutable and out of reach, the eucalyptus is the antipode of a long tradition of symbols drawn from nature whose unfurling has come to represent spiritual revelation. T.S. Eliot's poetry is full of such metaphorically rich figures: the "multifoliate rose" of "The Hollow Men" (91); the rose garden of "Burnt Norton," which conjures what Northrop Frye has called a world "full of elemental spirits" (153). And there is also, of course, the epiphanic climax of the *Four Quartets*, where the mystic intermingling of England and the descending spirit is expressed through lines that bear the cadence of liturgy:

> All manner of thing shall be well
> When the tongues of flame are in-folded
> Into the crowned knot of fire
> And the fire and the rose are one. (223)[3]

The topos of a natural unfurling representing a spiritual revelation can be traced throughout the English and American traditions. In *In Memoriam* Tennyson connects the presence of his dead friend's spirit with the trembling of "large leaves of the sycamore" (113); and Whitman attaches to his leaves of grass intimations of immortality, as he likens them to "the beautiful uncut hair of graves" (30). In what Harold Bloom cites as this topos's primal scene (101), the prophet Isaiah binds the idea of an unfurling leaf with that of spiritual revelation: "And all the host of heaven shall be dissolved, and the heavens shall be rolled together as a scroll; and all their host shall fall down, as the leaf falleth from the vine" (34:4). Here the connection between a loosening leaf (or bloom), the book (in this case a scroll), and the revelatory scene is made explicit. West only hints at this full symbolic structure in his first reference to eucalyptus leaves rustling, green and silver, in the breeze (*Day* 62). Following this reference, the promised revelatory scheme is stalled, silenced, as is Miss Lonelyhearts's urge to utter words of portent.

West introduces other motifs that intimate an apocalyptic movement, but which are not, ultimately, indicative of any form of revelation. Early in *The Day of the Locust* he describes the California night as being suffused "with a pale violet light" (61), and in the novel's concluding scene, "great violet shafts of light" beckon the crowds to Kahn's Persian Palace (175). Eleanor Cook has characterized violet as an apocalyptic colour, and we find support for her perception in Eliot's *The Waste Land*, where the poem's final section, depicting the West's decay, is envisioned amidst "Cracks and reforms and bursts in the violet air" (*Collected Poems* 77). But Eliot's cataclysm receives its blessing – however meagre – its ritualistic incantation conjuring a "Peace which passeth understanding" (86n). This cryptic intimation of revelation, expressed in the exotic language of the Upanishads and presenting an equation of faith more ambiguous than defined, sets Eliot's poem within the apocalyptic tradition that we have been tracing. *The Day of the Locust*, however, offers its reader no such comforting suggestion of a transcendental reality. The mêlée at Kahn's Persian Palace is breached by a very secular force – the Los Angeles Police Department – and as Tod is carried away by these mock saviours, he mimics their patrol car siren, as if he is cursed to remain a caller of portents and warnings, without any promise of relief or succour.

West makes use of explicit Eliotic references to cataclysm in a poem entitled "Burn the Cities," which appeared in *Contempo* in 1933. Like *The Waste Land*, West's poem envisions the razing of the world's great cities – Jerusalem, Paris, London – by cataclysmic fire. But as in *The Day of the Locust*, his vision eschews even the most subtle portents of revelation. Contemporary social decline and renovation are placed in a definitively secular context:

Workers of the World
Unite
Burn Paris

.   .   .   .   .

London will burn

It will burn
In the heat of tired eyes
In the grease of fish and chips
The English worker will burn it ... (Martin 330)

One even gets the impression that West is not truly concerned with the danger of secular cataclysm, as his poem of portent quickly descends into a parody of its own style and becomes a kind of sour joke:

Paris will burn easily
Paris is fat
Only an Eskimo could eat her
Only a Turk could love her
The Seine is her bidet
She will not hold urine
She squats upon the waters and they are oil ... (Martin 330)

These are no fragments shored against the ruins of a disaffected faith. Rather, "Burn the Cities" is more strongly parodic of the apocalyptic voice than emulative of it. Beginning with an invocation of the Eastern Star, a symbol central to Christian figurations of divinity, the poem descends into a pastiche of near-surrealist buffoonery.

In his treatment of apocalyptic vision in "Burn the Cities" and in *The Day of the Locust*, West makes use of a language of ontology and faith that no longer satisfies him. The guiding principle in both these works seems to be that modern man has been "stripped of his symbols of existential meaning" (Baird 386). Without their necessary complement of transfiguring light, the intimations of apocalypse in his novels are like tired ornaments, the remnants of a tradition that has failed. It is this condition, according to James Baird, that has led Western writers to fulfil an urge to usher in "a new era of symbols to be made from a new culture" (401). In *Miss Lonelyhearts*, West points to the East as a potential source of authentic myth and symbol. Miss Lonelyhearts's intrigue with *The Brothers Karamazov* and his monkish emulation of Father Zossima might represent nothing more than a simple fascination with normative Christian faith, but Baird characterizes Western man's fascination with Dostoyevsky's novel as being a more complex issue than this. He describes Herman Hesse's preoccupation with *The Brothers Karamazov* in the context of the failure of Western archetypes and conceives of Karamazov as representing the *russischer Mensch* – the incarnation of Eastern irrationality (424). Baird quotes Hesse, from a book that appeared in its English translation a decade before *Miss Lonelyhearts* was published: "The ideal of the Karamazoff ... Asiatic and occult, is already beginning to consume the European soul. That is what I mean by the downfall of Europe ... a turning back to Asia" (424). The curious monastic poses that Miss Lonelyhearts tries out and, even more fundamental, the grotesque iconography of trash and dream visions of a world in flux suggest that the faith that West's "priest of the Twentieth Century" pursues with such difficulty has the potential for being made from "a new era of symbols."

It is desperation – an obsessive urge to make something of his "dead" world – that brings on the "Religious Experience" in the novel's climactic chapter (56). And it may be Miss Lonelyhearts's desperation that accounts for the excesses of his experience: the rose, central to so many symbolic representations of the divine, makes its appearance with a vengeance. The room is "washed ... clean as the innersides of the inner petals of a newly forced rosebud," and the born-again newsman feels that his "heart was a rose and in his skull another rose bloomed" (57). But this bedroom conversion, brimming with traditional Western symbols of Christian revelation, quickly gives over to mockery. Considering his "new life," Miss Lonelyhearts plans to submit "drafts of his column to God" so God can approve them (57). Even the crucifix – the talisman upon which he meditates – has a chilling character. Described as "bright bait on the wall," it reminds us of the hooklike paraphernalia of grotesque visions, of lures that will catch at the skin of the most wary mystagogue.

This final "Religious Experience" is also noteworthy for the absence of the enigmatic, occultic motifs that appear throughout the novel. The world of secrets, of enigmatic mystery, has been discarded in favour of a more recognizable revelatory code. This "conversion," then, might be seen as the mystagogue's final loss of nerve. Miss Lonelyhearts's last spiritual turn ends as a grotesque pratfall, and the adept tumbles from his masterly perch at the top of a tenement stairway.

The enigmatic dreamscapes in *Miss Lonelyhearts* and the fever of irrational California-style mystagoguery in *The Day of the Locust* have much in common with the long tradition of apocalyptic art and literature. The Book of Revelation and its chimerical vision of the abyss, Bosch and his horrific landscapes, the apocalyptic writings of the Apocrypha, the irruption of the irrational in the religious vision of *The Brothers Karamazov* are all important precedents for West's curious mixture of cultural decay and yearning after the divine. But neither of his two short novels provides any form of transcendent vision in answer to their portrayal of the collapse of Western values. Tod Hackett is carried off by the Los Angeles police, and Miss Lonelyhearts's rosy vision is punctuated by that most secular of American salutes, a gun shot. Mystagogues will come and go, West seems to say, and the narrative of the end will be told and retold, no matter how stale the terms of its telling become. *Miss Lonelyhearts* and *The Day of the Locust* engage in an interpretive struggle with a symbolic authority and invoke a dialogue that renders apocalyptics – formerly a source of fearsome predetermination – a farcical fantasy. But the very serious outcome of such a struggle with narratives of inevitability is freedom.

8 An End to Endings: Saul Bellow's Anti-Apocalyptic Novel

A discussion of apocalyptic narratives – stories of the end – need not be limited to questions of literary symbolism and biblical sources. Our times have an apocalyptic tenor. We are constantly confronted by forms of belief and action no less antinomian and suspicious than those described by the French historian Jules Michelet as having flourished at the turn of the last millennium: "people were waiting. The prisoner waited in his dark dungeon ... the serf in his furrow ... The monk waited in the abstinences of the cloister, in the solitary tumults of the heart, in the midst of temptations and of remorse and curious visions, miserable plaything of the Devil" (qtd. in O'Brien 8). The Japanese are transfixed by a cult made up of young university graduates and trained scientists who, having abandoned their comfortable lives, follow a Rolls Royce–driving monk influenced by Buddhism and Hinduism who predicts the world will end amid an attack of sarin gas – a product that, it seems, he and his followers feverishly manufactured to make the prediction hold. In America a destroyed cult outpost on the Texan desert, named for a mountain in northern Israel, is increasingly seen as a site of witness, an early battlefield in an ongoing war between a satanic federal government and those who perceive themselves as recipients of divine prophecy.[1] A sign erected at Waco by a disgruntled sect member reads "Welcome – Worlds most persecuted church" (Verhovek 1).

Millennial endings, Frank Kermode tells us, inevitably produce an "apocalypse-crisis," a perception of a reigning decadence "associated with the hope of renovation" (*Sense* 9). Even the Pope, no cultist or paranoiac, is said to be "preparing himself" for "some apocalyptic announcement" in the year 2000 (O'Brien 37). But Jacques Derrida, in an article to which I will return entitled "Of an Apocalyptic Tone Recently Adopted in Philosophy," tells us that we need not look to periods of distinct historical transition for evidence of the influence of apocalyptics on the Western imagination. The West, he argues, "has been dominated" by "discourses of the end." "This is not only the end of this here," he writes, mimicking the tone used by a great many of those who have claimed to possess a mysterious secret and have announced, relying on their "eschatological eloquence," "I tell you this in truth; this is ... the end of history, the end of the class struggle, the end of philosophy, the death of God, the end of religions, the end of Christianity and morals ... the end of the subject, the end of man, the end of the West ... the end of the earth, *Apocalypse now*" (80). Here Derrida points to the influence that the apocalyptic mode has had on a wide range of discourses – the political, the philosophical, the literary, as well as on visionary religious writings.

In *Mr. Sammler's Planet*, Saul Bellow's 1970 novel confronting the Holocaust, the American Space Program, and the dedication of late-sixties youth to "experiencing the Age" (162), it is Mr Sammler's perception of a dangerous flirtation with apocalypticism that informs his response to his times. Sammler – a Holocaust survivor, a "man of seventy-plus" (3) – has strong opinions about the dangers of "eschatological eloquence":

Like many people who had seen the world collapse once, Mr. Sammler entertained the possibility it might collapse twice ... You could see the suicidal impulses of civilization pushing strongly. You wondered ... whether the worst enemies of civilization might not prove to be its petted intellectuals who attacked it at its weakest moments -attacked it in the name of proletarian revolution, in the name of reason, and in the name of irrationality, in the name of visceral depth, in the name of sex, in the name of perfect instantaneous freedom. For what it amounted to was limitless demand ... refusal of the doomed creature (death being sure and final) to go away from this earth unsatisfied. (33–4)

On Mr Sammler's planet in the early spring of 1969, shortly before the launching of Apollo xı, the prospect of a moon landing feeds an already end-directed view of the earth. "Of course," Sammler muses, "at the moment of launching from this planet to another something was ended, finalities were demanded, summaries" (277). The imminent presence of men on the moon fosters the belief in a new world, in an epoch of vastly different, if not heightened, possibility. When the Apollo spacecraft landed on the moon on 20 July 1969, President Nixon proclaimed that Americans were living through "the greatest week in the history of the world since creation" (Held 319).

Although Sammler admits the inevitability of the moonshot's eschatological flavour, he is ever mistrustful of the tendency to read current technological developments in apocalyptic terms. "I always hated people who declared that it was the end," he says. "What did they know about the end?" (304–5). But Sammler sees something more than naiveté and irrationality behind the urge to interpret the triumph of space travel as a great new beginning that will usher in the "end of things-as-known" (278). His belief, throughout Bellow's narrative, is that such interpretations are scripted, narrated, willed. The invocation of apocalyptic patterns is, according to Sammler, part of a conscious plan: "wasn't everything being done to make it intolerable to abide here," he asks, detecting what he calls "a scorched earth strategy. Ravage all ... Defile, and then flee to the bliss of oblivion" (135).

Here Bellow confronts his readers with the question of responsibility, with the possibility of an ethical alternative to apocalyptic narratives, and he prompts us to trace the motivation behind such narratives. Mr Sammler's musings suggest that we stop accepting the inevitability of a doomed ending and overcome our taste for the "flavor of the end of things-as-known" (278). Derrida presents a similar challenge: "Where do they want to come to, and to what ends, those who declare the end of this or that ... What effect do these noble, gentile prophets or eloquent visionaries want to produce? With a view to what immediate or postponed benefit? What do they do, what do we do in saying this?" ("Of an Apocalyptic" 82–3).

To answer these questions, we must look more closely at apocalypse as a "coherent and recognizable literary genre" (Collins, "Towards" 18). From there, we can examine what prompts the creation of such narratives, and further, what has lead to their tenacious hold on our imagination. If we accept, as I will propose, that stories of the end are fictions, then the end cannot be said to be an inevitability, a suprahuman truth, but a scenario that we construct and then enact. The end, it might be said, is not inevitable, but something for which we are responsible. Maurice Blanchot makes a similar point, using a more masterly tone: "Literature is more than a forgery – it is the dangerous ability to seek reality through the infinite multiplication of the imaginary" (224). Mr Sammler himself has his own clear belief in the powerful hold that certain narratives of social and political transformation have over us. Characterizing the influence of H.G. Wells, George Bernard Shaw, Karl Marx, and Jean-Jacques Rousseau, he describes them as "people who set the terms, who make up the discourse, and then history follows their words. Think of the wars and revolutions we have been scribbled into" (212–13).

The theologian John Collins tells us that apocalyptic writings developed as an expression of a "philosophy of life prevalent in the intertestamental period" ("Apocalyptic" 22). Jewish and early Christian writers were motivated by the need to "give hope to the faithful in time of oppression" and by a heightened belief in the onset of what Collins calls "a new world order" ("Apocalyptic" 28). The most important difference between apocalyptic writing and prophetic texts is that for the prophets, the "most significant action takes place on earth," while for the apocalypticists "the most significant action takes place between heavenly mythological beings, in the conflict of God and Belial, Christ and Anti-Christ, angels and demons, sons of light and sons of darkness" ("Apocalyptic" 30). Collins refers to this world-view as a "two-storey" universe, one in which "earthly biological life is not the highest form of experience for which human beings can hope. There is a whole higher realm of life" ("Apocalyptic" 37–8). In apocalyptic revelations a mystery or secret is most often "revealed by an angel," but occasionally a "human hero himself is said to travel in the heavenly realm," where, as in the Book of Enoch, a text associated with the Qumran sect, the mysterious movement of the stars is explained ("Apocalypse").

Recently, influential studies by Elaine Pagels, a professor of religion at Princeton University, have altered the scholarly focus on apocalyptic narrative by highlighting what she asserts is its most salient, as well as its most dangerous, characteristic. Pagels argues that apocalyptic writing developed as sectarian conflicts reached their height in biblical Israel, during the second century BCE (115). Dissident Jews, including the now-extinct Essenes and the followers of Jesus, denounced members of the Jewish establishment as "apostates," accusing them of "having been seduced by the power of evil [which they] called by many names: Satan, Belial, Mastema, Prince of Darkness" (108). Collins points to the centrality of narratives of cosmic war in apocalyptic texts, but does not link such narratives to any social or historical circumstances. Apocalyptic writing, Pagels concludes, is almost always – as with much sectarian literature – a genre reliant on demonization. It was the apocalypticists who elevated Satan – the *shatan*, who in biblical texts is an angelic emissary doing God's bidding – to the leader of an "evil empire" said to foment a cosmic war that mirrors the earthly battle between the godly and those who have subjected themselves to the rule of wickedness (Pagels 105, 112). Here, apocalyptic narrative, through its reliance on the twin themes of war between good and evil and the threat of satanic power, favours religious and social revolution, as well as a deep-set yearning for the end of an epoch of perceived decadence and the appearance of a new world cleansed from pollution.

There are a number of key similarities between traditional apocalyptic narrative and the terms within which the American Space Program was discussed. The moon, a heavenly secret, gave itself up to human discovery; in the conquest of this secret, according to Sammler, man dreamed of relinquishing "earthly biological life" (Collins, "Apocalyptic" 38) in favour of the possibility of life in a higher realm, a New Eden of "quiet colonies, necessarily austere" (Bellow, *Mr. Sammler* 53). Wernher von Braun, the German-trained rocket scientist who directed NASA's space program, described the Apollo landing as "the beginning of a process that will transfer human life to areas beyond the earth, which is ultimately doomed to extinction … Could it possibly be God's plan for men to spread the spark of life to other heavenly bodies?" (Held 319).

Von Braun and others in the American government also raised the spectre of apocalyptic war between America and the Soviets, arguing for the "significance of man's imminent conquest of space" and raising the threat that a Soviet victory would "inevitably" cost Americans "freedom itself" (Bergaust 304). The astronauts trained to lead this conquest, not unlike the "human heroes" of apocalyptic literature, learned through their travels the secrets of the heavenly realm. Men of science, as well as their supporters and promoters, became the new mystagogues, those who led the masses into a mystery; they led the crowd by way of "a small number of initiates gathered into a sect with a 'crypted' language" toward the hope of a heavenly life (Derrida, "Of an Apocalyptic" 69). As the unsettling outcome of emigration to the moon, Mr Sammler imagines an "oligarchy of technicians, engineers, the men who ran the grand machines" governing "vast slums" of the bohemian and abandoned (182).

One of the closing movements of Bellow's novel is a lengthy debate between Mr Sammler and a character he meets by chance, Professor Govinda Lal, a biophysicist whose work for NASA leads him to write a manuscript entitled "The Future of the Moon." Lal argues for the viability of human adaptation amid "exposed lunar conditions" (107) and insists that beneath the "superb PR" and "science-fiction entertainments" surrounding the space program, there lies a valuable, even transcendent, challenge: "The soul most certainly feels the grandeur of this achievement. Not to go where one can go may be stunting. I believe the soul feels it, and therefore it is a necessity" (217).[2] Having made this appeal to the soul, to humankind's visionary faculty, Lal insists that space travel need not be seen within an eschatological context; in his words, "it does not necessarily have to be a death-voyage" (219). But almost as soon as he speaks these words, he admits the inevitable connection in the contemporary imagination between the moon landing and the earth's doom:

Obviously we cannot manage with one single planet. Nor refuse the challenge of a new type of experience. We must recognize the extremism and fanaticism of human nature. Not to accept the opportunity would make this earth seem more and more a prison. If we could soar out and did not, we would condemn ourselves ... As it is, the species is eating itself up. And now Kingdom Come is directly over us and waiting to receive the fragments of a final explosion. Much better the moon. (219)

Mr Sammler's response to Lal's plea in favour of the "inventiveness" and "adventure" presented by space travel (217) includes an answer to Derrida's interrogation of those who "declare the end of this or that" ("Of an Apocalyptic" 82). What do they do, what do we do, when we predict the end of this world and the beginning of a new one? Sammler does not deny the atmosphere of ennui, of world-weariness, that surrounds him. He is no Pollyanna suggesting a more positive outlook. He describes New York City, his home since the end of the war, as a kind of capital of the end-of-things. With its soot-stained tulips, its "steaming sewer navels," and its "[s]palled sidewalks with clusters of ash cans," the city "makes one think of the collapse of civilization, about Sodom and Gomorrah, the end of the world. The end wouldn't come as a surprise here. Many people bank on it ... I am not sure that this is the worst of all times. But it is in the air now that things are falling apart, and I am affected by it" (9, 304).

Ultimately, however, Sammler addresses the apocalyptic tenor of the times to criticize it, not to further it. The Hebrew word *galah*, from which we get the Greek *apokalupsis*, does not suggest, as do all its translated forms, a fearsome catastrophe. It refers to a "disclosure," an unveiling of something hidden, and in this sense, Mr Sammler's musings on the implications of moon travel present us with a revelation: of the hidden narrative that lurks behind the triumph of technology and American know-how. Sammler suggests that, like all apocalyptic narratives, flight to the moon has its sectarian motivations, justified by the expectation of a coming ravagement that will separate the saved, who will "flee to the bliss of oblivion," abandoning the doomed (135). Narratives of transcendence – of escape from this earth in search of a life beyond death – cast their players in clearly delineated roles: those who will preside, priestly and blissful, over a new world order and those who must be left behind, inheritors of a "scorched earth" (135). Talk about whether the world is ending inevitably leads to discussion of death en masse, of an abstract death, which allows us to forgo real concern for particular deaths, those of the ones who are said to be doomed. Having once before fallen into the "category written off" – consigned to a Nazi mass grave – Mr Sammler knows how "humankind marks certain people for death. Against them there shuts a door" (230).

The stakes raised by the moon landing are very high, then. They include the expectation of ultimate devastation, of a housecleaning on earth even more grotesque in its completeness than the Nazis' apocalyptic mission to cleanse the world for "higher forms of human life [who, it was said, were] being dragged down and choked by lower forms" (O'Brien 82). For Sammler, the space program is a piece of "political showbiz" much crueller than such antique public spectacles as human sacrifice, witch hunts, or the Spanish church's autos-da-fé. By giving vent to the apocalyptic dreamings that are ever with us, it allows our "irrationalities to leave the sphere of dreams and come into the real world" (218–9). "Man now plays the drama," says Mr Sammler, "of universal death" (220). And one of the heroes of this drama – a new man free of earthly burdens and responsibilities – is the man in the moon. Who among us – each one a scribbler, a storyteller, an enactor of dramas – can say that the endings we create are of no account?

PART FOUR

The Collaborator

Forethought

In a compelling essay on the Rwandan genocide, Philip Gourevitch struggles to come to terms with the extent of the massacre and the nature of bystanders' complicity by recounting the story of Cain and Abel, one of the original cases of fratricidal murder: "The motive is political – the elimination of a perceived rival. When God asks what happened, Cain offers his notoriously guileless lie: 'I do not know; am I my brother's keeper?'" (86). This disingenuous line – one of the many central biblical phrases nearly turned into cliché through overuse – helps us to interrogate the tangled issues of responsibility among bystanders and collaborators during the Holocaust. The vulgarity of Cain's response, its plain inhumanity, arises from its easy dismissal of the ethical demand of responsibility for the other. The events of the Holocaust present us with a similar provocation: how would we act if we were in a position to choose between collaboration's ease and resistance? How great an impact would such an ethical demand have on us if an act of intervention placed our lives under certain threat? Would we remain silent, or write ingenuously and complacently of passing events? Or worse, would we favour them with our support? Of course, we cannot answer these questions in the abstract, but can discover our own inclinations only if the worst actually befalls us. Only then, with the ethical demand before us – palpable as Cain's weapon – might we discover who we are to another.

9 Warring with Shadows: The Holocaust and the Academy

The relationship between fascism and the Western intellectual tradition is one that continues to be dealt with ambivalently, with discomfort, and to some extent irresponsibly. Literary historians and critics rarely agree on the severity or consequent influence of a given writer's acts of collaboration. In some cases, the nature of the collaboration itself is disputed, as one commentator deems an act unforgivable, while another finds the same act excusable within its historical context. Such issues often define the way that scholars interpret the Nazi Holocaust, as well as the way in which they read the work of men and women who wrote during or following the war in Europe. The possible "taintedness" of a writer's œuvre is an issue that hovers in the background of much modern literary study. Without attempting to offer any final judgments concerning the way in which a community of readers should react to this taintedness, I will try in this chapter to examine how the fears and taboos that accompany any revelation of collaborationist acts skew scholarly efforts to contend with such acts.

I will use as a case study the unusually public and notorious debate that followed the revelation of Paul de Man's wartime writings in the summer of 1987, four years after his death. This debate was played out within the academic communities of North America, France, England, and Germany, as well as in the press, and in many ways continues to be an important reference point for literary scholars. The challenge of discovering exactly what de Man had done as a youthful collaborator and pamphleteer for the Belgium-based newspapers *Le Soir* and *Het Vlaamsche Land*, as well as a contributor to three other French-language bulletins, was quickly complicated by the use of the revelation by reporters and academics alike to smear deconstruction as a movement in contemporary thought. This smear campaign, along with a rather creepy tendency among de Man's students to worship their dead teacher, elicited an unpleasantly defensive response from many who may have been worthy, in a more level-headed atmosphere, of less biased, more probing analyses of the legacy of de Man's early writings. A common strand in scholarly discussions of his wartime journalism is the argument that contemporary journalists set out to destroy his reputation in order to put deconstruction in its grave. Derrida writes of the "ignorance, the simplism, the sensationalist flurry full of hatred which certain American newspapers displayed in this case" ("Like" 128). And Ortwin de Graef, who brought the wartime articles to public attention, sees in certain writers the desire to see the "defeat of deconstruction" ("Silence" 53). This dismissal of the responses of the American press as a kind of McCarthyite conspiracy further blurs the key elements of the debate.

I will focus on the most important responses to the de Man case in an effort to examine the ways in which thinkers who would otherwise be classed as leftists, or at least as theorists devoted to the critique of authoritarian ideologies, dealt with the revelation that one of their own had trafficked in what Jacques Derrida rightly calls "the very worst" ("Like" 132). My key points of reference will be de Man's wartime articles, most importantly those that appeared in *Het Vlaamsche Land*, an Antwerp daily, between March and October 1942. I have chosen to focus on these ten pieces because they have received considerably less attention than the articles that ran in *Le Soir*. I will also consider Derrida's long and, I think, ill-considered article "Like the Sound of the Sea Deep within a Shell: Paul de Man's War" and Shoshana Felman's "Paul de Man's Silence," along with reviews by literary scholars that appeared in journals of large and relatively general readership. Among these are Geoffrey Hartman's piece in the *New Republic* and Frank Kermode's review article, which first appeared in the *London Review of Books*.

Taking an overview of this field of response is much like gaining access to an busy e-mail discussion forum. Each article under consideration addresses the de Man articles in question, responding both to the dead scholar of Yale's Comparative Literature Program and to the other writers engaged in the debate. In the ensuing conversation between some of our most important critics, the act of collaboration – of giving voice to Nazi sympathies and declaiming against those who resisted the occupiers of France and Belgium – is not always the foremost concern being addressed. Derrida and Felman, most conspicuously, allow professional concerns, as well as their personal attachments to de Man, to distract them from political issues and from the opportunity to talk probingly about the relationship between fascism and the intellectual in our century. I would also argue that the German crimes – which, by the time de Man was composing his wartime writings, were public knowledge – take a secondary role in the consideration of what it was that de Man thought and wrote as a youth and in his later career. The Holocaust, in fact, is used (one might say, abused) as arguments are made that de Man – who, as is well known, never addressed his wartime writings – actually devoted a career to critiquing his own early fascination with fascist ideology.

An approach seldom taken by commentators on the de Man case – one which would have saved the discussion from the fruitless attacks and counter-attacks over deconstruction – is to ask how his early work stands within the larger context of writing by prominent critics, poets, novelists, and ideologues who embraced the fascist vision. Before there was a debate over the value of post-structuralism, we had the spectacle of Ezra Pound in what Charles Olson called a "Gorilla Cage," at Pisa (73); that of T.S. Eliot pleading – after the liberation of Auschwitz and Belsen – for a European order based on "the common tradition of Christianity" (122); the example of W.B. Yeats, Wyndham Lewis, and D.H. Lawrence exhibiting a fascination for fascist politics. The skeletons belonging to these illustrious moderns did not have to be dug out of any dark closet; they were eminently visible. Yet those who attack deconstruction for its figures of notoriety do not seem to feel that their own tradition of choice should fall under the same degree of suspicion. The question at hand must *not* be: Does deconstruction offer a valid political critique? There is no question that if practised with suitable engagement and a share of Sartrian good faith, it does so. The question must rather be of a still-partisan, but vastly different nature: What has been the effect of fascism on our intellectual and literary tradition, and in what way does our veneration of certain figures preclude us from making our own engaged and responsible commitments to purging this effect?

The writings which de Man contributed to Belgian publications between 1939 and 1943 fall into a well-documented category. George L. Mosse's *Germans and Jews: The Right, the Left, and the Search for a "Third Force" in Pre-Nazi Germany* provides us with ample material by which to read and recognize where de Man's political commitments stood in those years. Mosse argues that the tendency among intellectuals in Germany and western Europe to accept fascism was motivated by an urge to discover a "Third Force," an alternative to capitalism and Marxism. The bourgeois age, according to proponents of this Third Force, was characterized by a rootlessness brought on by a flight to centres of finance and manufacturing and by a breakdown in values caused by rampant individualism (Mosse 15). In its most extreme rendering, this fallen world appeared in the writings of Ferdinand Céline as a disease-ridden civilization in which "[n]aked struggle, human selfishness, and lust for material gain [were] the only realities" (Mosse 152). Mosse argues that "it seems clear that most intellectuals' commitment to fascism was based on a very real dilemma: after 1918 the society in which they lived did not seem to function well or even to function at all; its political and economic instability (which seemed to verge on collapse) had to be transcended" (147).

What arose in response to this need was a belief in a national mystique that called for "true camaraderie among men" (28), a return to "absolute values" that were symbolized by the land, by an adherence to a "mystical community" (12), and sometimes by the call for a conservative revolution that would "overthrow the present order" in favour of a "past uncontaminated by modernity" (15–16). This latter, more extreme expression of fascist desire showed itself most explicitly in the Nazi party and in certain tenets of Mussolini's platform. But as Mosse points out, youth movements throughout Europe, always more idealistic and extreme than their parent organizations, supported similar plans, whether such groups were free of, or under the yoke of, German occupation (23, 25). By concentrating on the German expression of fascist ideals through

Volkish and later Nazi ideology, Mosse points to the way in which the German fascist movement influenced and differentiated itself from movements in other countries. He notes, for instance, that all "fascism shared an organic world view and believed in a hierarchy defined in terms of service to the Volk or nation as exemplified by the leader" (26). On the other hand, he suggests that racism in general and anti-Semitism in particular were less rooted in the nationalist movements of western Europe than they were in Germany (28). To further qualify this distinction, he points to the centrality of the Jew as other within German fascist mythology: "the Jew became the foil for the evolution of this nationalism ... The Jew stood for the shallow and insincere adaptation to external reality, opposed to all that was true, genuine, and beautiful" (20).

As another point of reference, we should also take account of the French fascist heritage if we are to fully appreciate the atmosphere in which the work of intellectuals under German occupation developed. Although Mosse directs us to the German context as paradigmatic, Jeffrey Mehlman, in his *Legacies of Anti-Semitism in France*, refers to pre–Second World War French intellectual life as a "drama of Jewish exclusion" (4). The inception of this drama, he argues, is found in Édouard Drumont's *La France juive* (1886), among the most popular publications of its time, which attempted to "found left-wing ... anti-Semitism as *the* philosophy of French modernity" (6). Mehlman traces the role of anti-Semitism as "the great mythology" of the "burgeoning twentieth century" by examining the publications of Blanchot, Drieu La Rochelle, Brasillach, and Montherlant in influential journals such as *L'Insurgé*, *Réaction*, and *Combat*. Here, writers parroted what was a comfortable intellectual creed in the inter-war years: France was stagnant in contrast with the Nazi revolution; the national disease was a "desiccated intellectualism" (Golsan 29); the country's true enemy was the flood of foreigners and refugees who had arrived after 1918; one was obliged to oppose the excessive individualism and the flaccidity of democratic ideals that characterized modern France.

George Mosse analyses the output of intellectuals, men whose work it was to guide social, literary, and political discourse. Because of this choice, the expressions of fascist sympathy that he documents are by and large those of Germany's elites. Before I turn to a discussion of de Man's early writings, I will pair Mosse's presentation of the intellectual's use of fascist polemics with the employment of such rhetoric by the German Nazi party. One of the celebrated pre-war showplaces for Nazi political, aesthetic, and racial ideology was the notorious art exhibition, *Entartete Kunst*, or "Degenerate Art," which was organized in Munich in 1937. Some 16,000 paintings, sculptures, drawings, and prints (Barron 19), deemed alternatively "art-Bolshevism" (360), "barbarism of representation" (364), or simply "Jewish" art, were appropriated from German galleries and displayed in a newly renovated hall in central Munich. The show was touted as an official act of purgation of all avant-gardist influences in German art. Expressionism came in for special abuse from the show's organizers as an art form that courted "deliberate distortion," a "disregard for the basics of technique" (364), and a fascination with "mindless, moronic" faces (376). In his inaugural speech for the show, Hitler himself branded the Expressionists as "incompetents and charlatans" (368). The catalogue for "Degenerate Art" sounded the call for an ongoing Nazi "revolution" and for a concerted effort to put an end to the preceding "decades of cultural decadence" that had sullied the German Volk (360).

With these alternative points of reference – that of Mosse's intellectual community and that of the propagandistic Nazi assault on modern art – I turn to a discussion of de Man's early writings. A close reading of his articles in *Le Soir* and *Het Vlaamsche Land* reveals his early affiliations with a distinctly pro-German brand of rightist ideology. Throughout the writing which he did for *Het Vlaamsche Land*, a paper, it should be noted, that was set up by the occupying forces and printed with machinery expropriated from a censored newspaper in Antwerp (Hamacher, *Wartime* vii), French social and literary culture is compared negatively to that of Germany. In a review entitled "People and Books: A View on Contemporary German Fiction," de Man declaims that "the French artistic spirit has a less solid and firm basis than the German one" (HVL 20 August 1942), and in a later article he suggests that German literature could be characterized by the "presence" of "sociological insights," while French writing might be characterized by the "absence" of these (HVL 27–28 September 1942).[1] In somewhat broader statements, which must be deemed collaborationist in a time of occupation by outside forces, de Man repeatedly welcomes what he calls the "gradual growth of a European idea of unity" (HVL 31 May – 1 June 1942), and in a 1942 review of the work of German writer Ernst

Jünger, he remarks: "there is a lesson to be learned from Jünger's aesthetic tendency that cannot be repeated often enough: I mean the usefulness for a writer to be open to all expressions of Western civilizations, not to confine himself within local traditions" (HVL 26–27 July 1942).

These admonitions in favour of openness to other cultures – innocuous enough in times of peace and free cultural exchange – take on an undeniably ominous tone in times of occupation. And in an overtly collaborationist review of a Flemish pamphlet entitled *The Armistice: 1918–1940*, de Man fully supports the writer's opinion that the recent armistice arrangements made by Germany were carried out in a fashion "more dignified, more just and more humane" than those imposed by France in 1918. He urges Flemish readers to peruse this pamphlet in order to deepen their knowledge of "la doctrine nationale-socialiste" (LS 12–14 April 1941), and in an afterthought, he announces a forthcoming pamphlet that will speak of the marvels of the German chemical industry.

Even more serious, I think, than these tendencies to welcome the occupier's influence and cultural example is an inclination to mimic much of the ideological jargon that Mosse points to in his study of European fascism. Readers who have glanced at de Man's youthful essays and described them as having "no marked political bias" (Stengers 44) must contend with such remarks as the following, in a piece called "Contemporary Trends in French Literature" written in May 1942: "the war has exercised no influence on artistic creation ... For this war is not the cause of changes, but rather the result of an already existing revolution" (HVL 17–18 May 1942). By the time de Man wrote these words, some 30,000 German Jewish refugees had passed through Belgium, many of them moving on to France. Belgium's pre-war Jewish community had undergone a radical transformation. At the outbreak of the war it was numbered at roughly 90,000. By the end of 1940 only 52,000 remained, as both refugees from the Reich and Belgian citizens left their homes (Hilberg, *Destruction* 383–4). While de Man wrote so benignly of the German war effort, Jewish lawyers and civil servants were losing their positions, Jews were being registered for easier surveillance, many Jewish businesses had been Aryanized – the Nazi term for expropriation without recompense – Jews wore the yellow star, and "thousands of men between the ages of 16 and 60, as well as women from 16 to 40, were rounded up for forced labor in projects ... at

Audinghem and other areas" (Hilberg, *Destruction* 385–7). In the same article, reflecting on the outcome of the German occupation of France, de Man refers, in a rather sinister manner, to "material factors the object of which is not profound."

De Man makes further use of Nazi justifications for the war in the east, in a number of related references to the struggle with "extra-European forces" that threatened "representatives of continental civilization" (*HVL* 31 May – 1 June 1942). It is unclear whether his reference to "extra-European forces" is meant to evoke Bolshevism – as the expression of an Asian culture – or Judaism. But on the basis of the repeated pairing of these two forces in Nazi and other fascist propaganda, de Man might well mean to invoke both. What is most troublesome about such comments is that they make use of the most specious of German (and in our own time, revisionist) arguments in support of cultural imperialism and genocide. This characterization of the war as a clash between "continental civilization" and "extra-European forces" appears in an article written in 1942, which states most clearly de Man's sense of the intellectual's role in the political and social affairs of Europe under Nazi occupation. The "present revolution," he writes,

forces an important task upon today's intellectual elite, a task which cannot be accomplished by the will of the people but only by the knowledge and study of the few ... we can point out the fact of the cultural division that governed these last years of the liberalist era ... When even in the serene realms of knowledge there can be no agreement or mutual understanding, it is no wonder that, on the level of practical questions, we are confronted with a veritable chaos.

During the last few years, people of value and significance, who up to then had only occupied themselves with specialized research or individual artistic expression, have finally seen this. They have understood that it had become an urgent necessity to bring together such attempts, which were scattered all over this continent. Spiritual life could no longer go its own way indifferently ... it became its duty to unite the creative forces of all European states.

And as soon as they realized this, they reached the insight that actually there had never been a deep division and that, unconsciously, the same tendencies and evolutions had occurred in all countries. (*HVL* 31 May – 1 June 1942)

This passage borrows its logic from the rhetoric common to European fascist thought of the inter-war period. The failure of democratic society had lead, it was argued, to "veritable chaos," and the call to "[s]piritual life" – the pursuit of a mystical community of true camaraderie and right values – was repeatedly proposed as Europe's cure. Undoubtedly, de Man's sense of the ongoing evolution, of the "revolution" carried out "[d]uring the last few years," cannot be said to refer to anything other than the Nazi accomplishments in Germany and abroad. It is rather unpleasant, but not, I think, surprising, to find that Hitler, in his inaugural speech at the Munich opening of "Degenerate Art," spoke as well of a "living evolution" (Barron 384) that would overcome the "total failure" of the previous era's artistic and social movements by asserting art that would be true to the way in which the German people "really see and feel" (Barron 384, 386).

De Man's undoubtedly more sophisticated sense of the past decades' failure is expressed at greater length in an article entitled "People and Books. A View on Contemporary German Fiction" (*HVL* 20 August 1942). In this piece the opinions expressed bear an uncanny similarity to those put forward by the curator of "Degenerate Art":

When we investigate the post-war literary production in Germany, we are immediately struck by the contrast between two groups, which, indeed, were also materially separated by the events of 1933. The first of these groups celebrates an art with a strongly cerebral disposition, founded upon some abstract principles and very remote from all naturalness. The theses of expressionism, though very remarkable in themselves, were used here as tricks, as skillful artifices aimed at easy effects ... as a pretext for a forced, caricatured representation of reality. Thus, [the artists of this group] came into an open conflict with the proper traditions of German art which had always and before everything else clung to a deep spiritual sincerity. Small wonder, then, that it was mainly non-Germans, and specifically jews, who went in this direction ...[2]

Nevertheless, there was another group at work in Germany, which did not give in to this aberrant fashion ... For Dutch publishers and translators a source of riches can be found there which has not yet been sufficiently exploited. In this way they could offer their compatriots the possibility to get acquainted with authors who have remained true to their natural disposition, despite the seductiveness of scoring cheap successes by using imported formulas. (*HVL* 20 August 1942)

De Man's characterization of Expressionism as cerebral, abstract and remote from nature and things spiritual – as a product of ersatz modernism – echoes the fascist hatred of all things "artificial" and "shallow" as representing the "conspiratorial menace of modernity" (Mosse, *Germans* 9, 20, 154).

Derrida's reaction to de Man's wartime articles is stated in very personal terms – as an elegiac remembrance of a friend, as well as a collective battle-cry in support of colleagues under siege. "Like the Sound of the Sea Deep within a Shell: Paul de Man's War" transforms the discussion from an analysis of the nature of his collaboration into a defensive manœuvre in response to the "war" against deconstruction.[3] Derrida begins his essay by directing it at a very limited audience: "For what is happening with these 'revelations,'" he writes, "is happening to *us*" (128). Further, the press is said to be waging a "deadly war" based on a "dream of killing the dead in order to get at the living" (128).

Derrida's essay raises a problem that will resonate throughout the discussions of de Man's wartime writing, that is, the question of who has read what. At the time of writing, he had read only 25 of the 170 articles that de Man published in *Le Soir* (131), albeit the most crucial ones, handpicked by the Belgian researcher who discovered them. He had also read French translations of 4 of the 10 articles that appeared in *Het Vlaamsche Land*, including "Content of the European Idea," with its mid-1942 call for European unity and the intellectual's responsibility to follow a "[s]piritual" path away from the "chaos" of recent years and its condemnation of "extra-European forces" said to be preying on "continental civilization" (*HVL* 31 May – 1 June 1942). Derrida had also seen the piece entitled "Literature and Sociology," with its denigration of French literature in favour of the German tradition exemplified by Ernst Jünger (*HVL* 27–28 September 1942). Derrida is uncharacteristically ingenuous in his analysis of these articles. He makes little effort to relate their discourse to that which was common among German and other Western intellectuals before the war, and he intimates that de Man used such terms as "the present revolution" (*HVL* 31 May – 1 June

1942) with no clear intention – as part of a rhetorical "maze" whose outcome could not be seen (136).

Derrida's main point with regard to the articles that he had read is to assert that ambivalence and a lack of political engagement characterized de Man's early writings, that the essays present themselves as strongly self-questioning documents, which are suspicious of authoritative ideologies and therefore prescient of the writer's mature method. In a sweeping generalization, referring to the articles' "massive effect" (134), he argues that "de Man's discourse is constantly split, disjointed, engaged in incessant conflicts ... all the propositions carry within themselves a counterproposition: sometimes virtual, sometimes very explicit, always readable, this counterproposition signals what I will call ... a *double edge* and a *double bind*" (135).

I will deal with this claim on two levels: as an interpretive response stated as an actual description of the articles and as a theoretical, or ideological, move. As an interpretive response, I would suggest that it is without evidence and wishful to the extent that one must say that Derrida is reading backwards, looking too hard for the methods and mastery of the mature de Man in his far less sophisticated early work. As a theoretical claim, the assertion finds Derrida practising the kind of deconstructive reading for which his less-brilliant students are often derided, but which I have never encountered him offering anywhere else in his own work. His method has always been to mark the inner contradictions, the failure of argument and logic in the foundation works of the Western metaphysical and literary traditions. Deconstruction is at its best, as Dominick LaCapra has pointed out, when it is in pursuit of covert "counterpropositions" in strong texts, the places where such texts contest themselves. I would argue that de Man's early articles do not in any way deserve to be characterized as strong works, worthy of the same philosophically rigorous reading as those of Levinas, Heidegger, or Rousseau. In contrast, the articles may simply be, as Sartre so effectively put it, beneath the dignity of literature, since, while in the service of oppression, they traffic in arguments that deny the freedom of men and women (46–7). In this way, "Like the Sound of the Sea Deep within a Shell" provides an unwitting parody of Derrida's otherwise powerful method. In a hurried effort to protect deconstruction from those who would "exploit" (155) the opportunity to smear it, he overdetermines the de Man articles, finding in them philosophical ambivalence and irony that is patently not present.[4]

Although Derrida goes to great lengths to eulogize and celebrate de Man as a friend, the weight of his article leans toward an appreciation of de Man's writings. Shoshana Felman's response to the wartime articles is even more problematic than Derrida's, since it not only vindicates de Man's journalism, but also strives to characterize him as a victim himself, as one who "in his later writings and his teaching ... does nothing other than testify to the complexity and ambiguity of history as Holocaust" ("Paul" 720). Her response to the de Man case, entitled "Paul de Man's Silence," appeared in *Critical Inquiry* in the summer of 1989, roughly a year after Derrida's essay was published in that journal. Felman provides little close reading of the articles themselves, concentrating instead on a complex analysis of the similarities that she sees between de Man's wartime experience and the narrative predicaments presented in *Moby-Dick* and Rousseau's *Confessions*. Her essay enacts a kind of canonization, a mythicization of a figure whom she sees, after the language of Melville, as one of the "metaphoric captains – leaders, mentors, or role models" (704).

The process by which de Man receives his elevation is traditional – through a typological reading of his work and his relationship to seminal texts. *Moby-Dick* is invoked in an effort to mark de Man as an Ishmael-like figure who broke painfully with his past, abandoning a family and his native Europe to atone for the essays that he wrote for *Le Soir*. By way of this break, according to Felman, he *"survives*, that is, not as the same but as a radically transformed Other" (718–19; emphasis mine). This mystical connection between de Man and Ishmael, based on the fact that de Man completed a translation of *Moby-Dick* into Flemish, is the first context in which the experience of survivorhood is ascribed to the erstwhile collaborator. According to Felman, "What survives is not the memory" of de Man's collaborative acts, but his experience "witnessing" the acts of violence that surrounded him and led him to be "entrapped, with no possibility of escape and with the war closing in on him" (719, 736n, 739).

In answer to questions about de Man's subsequent silence – his decision not to publicize the import of his writings during the war – Felman turns to a reading of Rousseau's *Confessions*, to set Rousseau's autobiographical account of an excuse made for a wrong done against de Man's inability to offer an excuse for his actions during the war. Felman contends that de Man's refusal to make an excuse for his acts in occupied Belgium constitutes a refutation of all excuses: "But how can one *absolve* the mystified historical collaboration with the Nazis? If the act of the journalistic collaborationist writing was, in a sense, a lie, would not the linguistic act of the confession – in recapitulating language as a straightforward referential witness, and in claiming to relieve or 'overcome guilt ... in the name of truth' – simply amplify and magnify the lie?" (729).

This urge to mythicize de Man – to draw his life in the large, heroic strokes of epic fiction – is evident throughout Felman's essay. More problematic, however, is her effort to redraw her ex-colleague as a *victim* of the war, or at least as a *survivor*, in the face of those who would pass judgment on him and mark him as a collaborator. To do this, Felman makes rather dubious use of the work of Primo Levi, primarily *The Drowned and the Saved*, which appeared prior to his suicide. I will quote Felman's use of Levi in full, since she introduces his work to counter what she sees as a typical "blindness" to history in the attacks on de Man: "'Popular history,' writes Primo Levi, 'and also the history taught in schools, is influenced by [a] Manichean tendency, which shuns half-tints and complexities: it is prone to reduce the river of human occurrences to conflicts, and the conflicts to duels – we and they, ... winners and losers, ... the good guys and the bad guys, respectively, because the good must prevail, otherwise the world would be subverted'" (706). Felman quotes further, without acknowledging the context of the discussion from which she draws these passages: "As Primo Levi testifies, 'The world into which one was precipitated was terrible, yes, but also indecipherable: it did not conform to any model; the enemy was all around but also inside, the "we" lost its limits, the contenders were not two, one could not discern a single frontier but rather many confused, perhaps innumerable frontiers, which stretched between each of us'" (706).

Here Felman argues for our inability to judge de Man by quoting, out of context, two passages describing life in the Lager, as Levi calls Auschwitz, and by using these passages to characterize de Man's predicament as a writer of articles for newspapers under Nazi control. By giving the impression that Levi's words are meant to evoke a generalized state of discomfort experienced by the average

European during the war, she not only does an injustice to his insistence on the uniqueness of life in the Lager, but she also misrepresents his careful effort to differentiate between those who were victims and those who were not. For Levi the two previously quoted passages describe, not a generalized European predicament, but "the network of human relationships inside the Lagers" (*Drowned* 37). "Let us confine ourselves to the Lager," he adds, in an attempt to prevent his readers from misinterpreting him (42), and he goes on to describe, in that singular community, a "gray zone" where he recognizes among the inmates "two camps of masters and servants" which "diverge and converge. This gray zone possesses an incredibly complicated internal structure and contains within itself enough to confuse our need to judge" (42).

Levi's point, then, is that among the inmates of the Lager, there were those who were "saved" by virtue of their ability to "organize" – in the argot of the camp – to take advantage of their weaker compatriots to ensure that they themselves would not be "drowned." He, by definition, was one of those who was saved. By using this context to discuss de Man – who was never interned or punished or deterred from his daily pursuits, but who, rather, wrote uncritically and at times favourably of the process of internment and punishment that was being carried out across western and central Europe – Felman blurs historical roles in a manner similar to that which Levi derides in a response to Liliana Cavani's film *The Night Porter*:

[Cavani] was asked to express briefly the meaning of a beautiful and false film of hers, [and] declared: "We are all victims or murderers, and we accept these roles voluntarily. Only Sade and Dostoevsky have really understood this." She also said she believed "that in every environment, in every relationship, there is a victim-executioner dynamism more or less clearly expressed and generally lived on an unconscious level."

I am not an expert on the unconscious and the mind's depths, but I do know that few people are experts in this sphere and that these few are the most cautious. I do not know, and it does not much interest me to know, whether in my depths there lurks a murderer, but I do know that I was a guiltless victim and I was not a murderer. I know that the murderers existed, not only in Germany, and still exist, retired or on active duty, and that to confuse them with their victims is a moral disease or an aesthetic affectation or a sinister sign of complicity; above all, it is precious service rendered (intentionally or not) to the negators of truth. (*Drowned* 48–9)

Felman's influential response to the de Man affair had a second life as a pivotal part of the 1992 volume *Testimony: Crises of Witnessing in Literature, Psychoanalysis, and History*. In this collection she prepares her reader for the revised version of "Paul de Man's Silence," now called "After the Apocalypse: Paul de Man and the Fall to Silence," with a lengthy introductory chapter describing a course that she taught at Yale entitled "Literature and Testimony." Her students read Camus, Dostoevsky, Mallarmé, Freud, and Paul Celan and concluded the course by watching two videotaped testimonies of Holocaust survivors from Yale's Video Archive for Holocaust Testimonies. The course made steady progress, examining the development of testimony as a literary genre, until "it broke out into a crisis" following the viewing of the accounts of two camp survivors (*Testimony* 47). After this experience, Felman argues, the class itself encountered the *trauma* of the Holocaust event and was forced, in its way, to purge this trauma or relive it, as do survivors themselves.

Felman has an unpleasant habit of letting such terms as "survivor," "witness," and "testimony" slip, so that they take on an all-purpose character: one who listens to the recounting of "extreme-limit-experiences" is referred to as a witness. Her students are said to be confronted with the task of "surviving the first [video] session." And Felman attends to her student's crisis by suggesting that "the significance of the event of your viewing of the first Holocaust videotape was, not unlike Celan's own Holocaust experience, something akin to *a loss of language*" (*Testimony* 49–50). Undoubtedly, part of her intention is to impart to her students a feeling of empathy for the victims of Nazi violence. But in effect, this introductory chapter supports the notion that *all of us* have been traumatized and are victims of the violence done to Western culture. As one reads from "Education and Crisis, or the Vicissitudes of Teaching," toward Felman's revised version of the well-known "Paul de Man's Silence," it is difficult not to see the former essay as preparatory material developed to support Felman's master narrative, in which de Man is portrayed as a heroic victim and witness whose writings do "nothing other than testify to the complexity and ambiguity of history as Holocaust" (Felman, "Paul" 720).

One cannot help but feel that Felman's use, in the rest of *Testimony*, of the work of Camus, Melville, Rousseau, and Walter Benjamin in support of de Man's dedication "to bearing witness" is revisionist in its own way. Free-associative, based on no documents (Felman refers to no letters or lectures to support her thesis about de Man's intentions), these readings stand on her rhetorical skill alone. Quite understandably, in the summer of 1989 Felman found herself in crisis and acted out by publishing an essay that turns on a sophistic reading of history aimed at preserving Paul de Man's position as one of America's pre-eminent scholars. It is baffling to think that a critic of her stature did not use the ensuing years to reconsider some of the more bizarre conclusions of this essay, and further, that she has gone to the trouble of developing intricate, one might even say ingenious, readings of some of our most important literary works to lend her rather single-minded thesis greater currency.

The last two articles that I will address – Frank Kermode's "Paul de Man's Abyss" and Geoffrey Hartman's "Blindness and Insight" – are of a different status from those by Derrida and Felman. As literary journalism that appeared in mass-market publications, they are in some way ephemera, although of a very special kind. Written by experts who hold a certain power over opinion, appearing in forums regarded as arbiters of taste and good judgment, these articles are meant to survey the field. Neither writer is motivated by the urge to enact damage control by way of the kind of wishful interpretations of history used by Derrida and Felman. Both Kermode and Hartman say what must be said. They condemn the anti-Semitic character of the writings, and they note the similarities between de Man's journalistic polemic and that of Europe's fascist right. My unease with these more honest responses arises from their tone. They react to de Man's rhetoric in a manner too muted, in a vein too dispassionate, and further, without any serious note of condemnation. The culminating effect of reading the entire œuvre of de Man's wartime articles is one of nausea. The ease with which he brought the spirit of bonhomie to the assertion that the weight of destiny drove Nazi policy in the realms of race, militarism, and social policy is appalling. In 1941, as the machinery of annihilation was being set up in Brussels and Antwerp, the youthful columnist celebrated the "humane" revolutionary reforms of Nazi policy (LS 12–14 April 1941) and, more notoriously, asserted that the lack of Jewish influence on modern European literature lead one to believe that "the creation of a Jewish colony isolated from Europe, would not entail deplorable consequences for the literary life of the West. The latter would altogether lose some personalities of mediocre value and would continue, as in the past, to develop in accordance with its great evolutionary laws" (LS 4 March 1941).

It is not enough to note, as Professor Kermode does, that we find only a "fairly low" level of anti-Semitism in these articles ("Paul" 106). Nor is it useful to characterize them, in Hartman's words, as "polite," not "vulgar ... by the terrible standards of the day" (26, 29).[5] And it is much worse blandly to suggest, as Derrida does, that it is better that de Man was not forced to contend with the revelation of his wartime writings. "It would have taken his time and energy. He did not have very much and that would have deprived us of a part of his work" ("Like" 150).

The tone of these admonitions is somehow inappropriate, not the voice of engagement that must answer to such acts in good faith. Sartre may still tell us the most, in *What Is Literature?*, about how we must respond to texts, such as the early de Man writings, that are in the service of the oppressor. "The work is never limited to the painted, sculpted, or narrated object," he writes in 1947. "We follow the red path which is buried among the wheat much farther than Van Gogh has painted it" (40). In the same way, we follow the path of de Man's early writings, and we find ourselves at the gate of the most terrible place that Europe has seen. We must admonish ourselves in the very terms that Sartre chose for a Europe only just emerging from the war. Of the reader's relationship to a work he writes, "You are perfectly free to leave that book on the table. But if you open it, you assume responsibility for it" (34). And to this observation I must offer my agreement with Sartre's imperative that if I find in this book the "world with its injustices, it is not so that I may contemplate them coldly, but that I may animate them with my indignation" (45).

Amid the flood of scholarly and journalistic work that has appeared concerning de Man's early writings, the most probing response may be found in Alice Kaplan's memoir *French Lessons*, which takes as its focus her experience of learning and teaching French, but which raises as well the author's personal involvement in the events surrounding the discovery of de Man's early writings. Kaplan studied at Yale when de Manian deconstruction was at its height, but had little contact with her department's rising literary star. De Man, she remembers, "seemed the least interested of anyone on the faculty" in her plans to write a doctoral thesis on "the problem of the fascist intellectual" (174). As a teacher he "failed" her, Kaplan writes, "only it was a failure that I wasn't aware of" (173–4). Unlike other commentators who recast de Man's silence concerning the war years as a refutation of all excuses, she perceives it as a dead loss:

I didn't go to talk to him, because I had no idea that he had given a minute's thought to the problem that interested me most – the problem of the fascist intellectual ... Think of the questions I could have asked him, had I known to ask: Why did he think intellectuals had been attracted to fascism? Had he been attracted, or had he been doing hack work? What was it like to write for a newspaper controlled by the Nazis? What did he know about the camps? What role did personality play in people's attitude toward fascism? How did listening to the radio and going to the movies alter their perception of the world? What was it like living through the purge of the fifties? How did his guilt affect him? (174)

Looking back on the article that she contributed to the discussion surrounding the wartime journalism, Kaplan chides herself for having taken a stance of "cool disinterest" motivated by a sense of scholarly decorum, rather than giving voice to the indignation that she felt, which was in part fuelled by her work on the broader connection between fascism and intellectuals (170). In *French Lessons* she offers an interpretation of de Man's journalism that differs from that of Derrida, Felman, and other influential commentators who spoke out on the subject: "I got the bound volumes of *Le Soir*, with de Man's articles in them. Under his by-line was every fascist cliché, every inane argument ... about the New Europe: one month, a glowing reference to futurism as the poetry of the New Europe: the next, a joke about Céline. There were distinctions within the collaborationist rhetoric that showed he was discerning, even as he was toeing the line" (168).

Kaplan's portrait of a young scholar unable to talk with her illustrious teacher about the events of the war mirrors the more general difficulty of confronting the work of writers and artists perceived to be tainted by collaborationist acts. Such biographical facts, as Geoffrey Hartman has written, tend "to devour all other considerations" (qtd. in Esch 31). In another fascinating set piece, Kaplan describes the time she spent with "the only fascist intellectual discussed in my dissertation who was still alive; his name was Maurice Bardèche. Bardèche was the keeper of the archives of the executed writer Robert Brasillach ... At the end of the war Bardèche, like Brasillach, was arrested and imprisoned. He had been a tenured professor at the University of Lille; he was stripped of his title ... He denounced the Jews; he doubted the truth of the Holocaust" (French 186).

Bardèche's résumé reads nothing like de Man's, but Kaplan's description of her struggle to confront him, to uncover a ground on which a dialogue might be held, provides us with an instructive scene against which to temper our own response to Paul de Man's wartime journalism. She neither suggests censoring Bardèche nor does she devise excuses for him. Like many of the writers we have discussed here, Kaplan insists on the necessity of examining how past worlds affect our own: "why does it feel so close, why am I still fighting the battles of another time and place, as though they were mine?" (199). With such questions in mind, we can not be in danger of losing sight of the source of our indignation or our potential for empathy.

Conclusion:
In Search of a Multicultural
Tradition

In the essays collected here I have not tried to characterize each
author as being representative of a Canadian or an American Jewish
tradition. Instead, I have attempted to make use of historical and
critical terms that address the way in which each author contends
with identity and memory, with continuity and loss. To conclude
my study I would like to discuss Jewish North American writing
in a broader context, to examine its relationship with the larger
cultural landscape. Here I will try to point to the distinct manner
in which Jewish writing has been received by mainstream American
and Canadian critics and readers, as well as to contrast this reception with that of writing by other groups whose literary output has
been called – in this century of ocean crossings and forced exiles –
"minority," "ethnic," or more recently, "multicultural" writing.

Michael Greenstein argues in the introduction to his *Third Solitudes: Tradition and Discontinuity in Jewish-Canadian Literature*, that
the "New York Intellectuals ... (Rahv, Trilling, Kazin, Howe, Fiedler,
Podhoretz) lent visibility and voice to Jewish-American writing:
having interpreted modernism to Americans, they helped pave the
way for Bellow, Malamud, and Roth to enter the mainstream" (4–
5). Greenstein quickly adds that "no similar critical mediation
occurred in Canada" (5). Although Canadian Jewish writers have a
popular following, are commonly taught in university courses, and
can now be seen to write out of a tradition that is at least three

generations old, the popularity and influence of their work has rarely been discussed in terms of its particularity – with attention to the ways in which Jewish culture and tradition account for the kind of writing they produce. This reception raises questions about the relationship between literature and history: How important is it for readers to understand the cultural context out of which a novelist writes? What is the outcome of critical studies of Jewish writing that read novels and poetry using only the canonical literary tradition as a framework? In what way has the "mainstreaming" of Jewish literature – the tendency to discuss it as a thoroughly integrated component of an established Canadian tradition – prevented a deeper study of the problematics and particularities of Jewish Canadian identity?

To answer these questions, we might briefly consider the quite different approach taken toward writing by Canadians whose work is included in a tradition called post-colonial literature. Just as Greenstein suggests that the New York Intellectuals offered an interpretation of post-war culture that allowed for a careful reading of Roth, Bellow, and Malamud, Canadian critics have done an excellent job of interpreting the work of Michael Ondaatje, Rohinton Mistry, Bharati Mukherjee, and a variety of other writers whose work can be viewed through the prism presented by the complicated interrelation of colonizer and colonized. This frame of reference has obvious relevance for contemporary Canadian discussions surrounding issues of identity, bilingualism, and multiculturalism, and since these issues have consistently remained at the forefront of public discussions, it is no surprise that literary critics have pursued a critical and canonical tradition that "requires us to pay very careful attention to the category of nation" and the way in which different kinds of nationalism are presented by contemporary authors (Brydon 9).

Leading Canadian critics, among them Diana Brydon, Linda Hutcheon, and W.H. New, have in many ways defined post-colonial writing for audiences in Canada and abroad; their discussion of the impact of colonialism on Canadian tradition has deepened our sense of what is at stake when we imagine a "Canadian mosaic," and further, what the more serious limitations are of the multicultural ideal. Brydon writes that many of the "sharpest debates" concerning Canadian pluralism "centre on the problem of how to situate and evaluate the cultural production of invader-settler colonies such as

Canada," and she points to a "current renegotiating of Canada and Canadianness" taking "place within a postcolonial context" (2, 1).

It might be argued that this is the context within which much discussion of the potential of Canadian multiculturalism has taken place in recent years, and further, that this particular context has not proved particularly fruitful for a consideration of the role of Jewish writing in Canada. But Brydon and Janice Kulyk Keefer have also contributed to a rethinking of the Canadian multicultural ideal by raising the possibilities of what they call "transcultural" writing. By this they mean narratives that have a "dynamic potential of cultural diversity, the possibility of exchange and change among and within different ethnocultural groups" (Kulyk Keefer, "From Mosaic" 14). For Kulyk Keefer, transcultural writing

sets as its priorities the crossing rather than defending of boundaries, the exploration rather than essentializing of otherness and difference; the exchange of information and sharing of experience, rather than the preserving of established rituals and prescriptive attitudes for the purposes of barring "outsiders." Transcultural texts engage with [a] multicultural ideal by foregrounding or revealing their authors' liminal position between two or more different countries, communities, cultures. ("Memory" 5)

Here we find a framework for considering what might be called scenes of cultural crossing, for an examination of the way that different communities' experiences and narratives confront and influence one another. It is just this sort of dynamic of exchange between Jewish writers in Canada and a broader tradition that has been little discussed. Much work has been done on lines of inheritance, on the centrality of A.M. Klein to the flowering of poetic careers of men and women born after him, but we still lack what might be called a transcultural reading of Jewish Canadian literature, which would provide a clear sense of the peculiarities of its reception and of its entanglement with Canadian culture.

But how can we relate the idea of a transcultural tradition to North American Jewish writing? How can we rethink the multicultural ideal in a way that will allow us to recognize the interplay between Jewish literature and the broader tradition? To do this, I think, we must see the multicultural ideal in different terms. We must reimagine it as a transcultural drama, focusing on the ways in which writers find themselves in a "liminal position," caught between two or more different countries, communities, or cultures. The cultural crossings brought about by the institutions of colonialism have been carefully theorized; one might even say that they have been institutionalized in North American universities under the rubric of "post-colonial studies." But far less has been done to uncover the surprising connections, correlations, paradoxes, and juxtapositions that have evolved from the points of confluence between émigré Jewish European culture and North American traditions. To draw our attention to such juxtapositions, I would like to recount two anecdotes which might be called foundation myths of multiculturalism and which offer narratives that place the ideal's conception in a vivid – one might contend, specifically Jewish North American – context.

It is arguable that the discovery of the potential of multiculturalism dates back to a particular historical and cultural moment, brought about by the meeting of European (and in important cases, Jewish) émigré anthropologists and surrealists in Manhattan during the Second World War. During his wartime stay in Manhattan, the anthropologist Claude Lévi-Strauss was overwhelmed by the variety of "preserved customs and stories" he encountered that represented cultures already vanishing "in the old countries." Among these were

the performances that we watched for hours at the Chinese opera under the first arch of the Brooklyn Bridge, where a company that had come long ago from China had a large following. Every day, from midafternoon until past midnight, it would perpetuate the traditions of classical Chinese Opera. I felt myself going back in time no less when I went to work every morning in the American room of the New York Public Library. There, under its neo-classical arcades and between walls paneled with old oak, I sat near an Indian in feather headdress and a beaded buckskin jacket – who was taking notes with a Parker pen. ("New York" 266–7)

In a similar vein, Roman Jakobson describes how the German-born American anthropologist Franz Boas often spoke of a Kwakiutl man who had come to work with him in New York:

Boas loved to depict the indifference of this man from Vancouver Island toward Manhattan skyscrapers ("we built houses next to one another, and you stack them on top of each other"), toward the Aquarium ("we throw such fish back in the lake") or toward the motion pictures which seemed tedious and senseless. On the other hand, the stranger stood for hours spellbound in the Times Square freak shows with their giants and dwarfs, bearded ladies and fox-tailed girls, or in the Automats where drinks and sandwiches appear miraculously and where he felt transferred into the universe of Kwakiutl fairy-tales. (142)

These scenes of cultural crossing do in fact have the magical texture of fairy tales; they convey a sense of modern imaginations exploding with new connections, correlations, paradoxes, and juxtapositions. The recollections of Lévi-Strauss and Boas provide rich evidence for the potential of the multicultural world-view and convey the range of historical, social, and cultural forces that converged to create the possibility for transcultural experience that motivated artists and critics to search for new forms suited to rendering their discoveries. In *The Predicament of Culture*, James Clifford refers to André Breton, Max Ernst, and Yves Tanguy – surrealist contemporaries of Lévi-Strauss – as "anthropological flâneurs," expatriates in flight from the war in Europe who devoted much of their exile in Manhattan to an excited search through dealers' closets for "pre-Columbian, Indian, Oceanic, or Japanese art" (238).

What, then, are the social and cultural forces at play in the above portraits of anthropological (or might we say, multicultural) *flâneurs*? Boas and Lévi-Strauss were both fascinated by the cultural other and the challenge of recounting the extremes of cultural interaction, yet they stand at some remove, retreating into a professional pose of objective appraisal rather than true dialogue. The "Indian" at work in the New York Public Library and Boas's Kwakiutl friend are each seen in terms that might also be used to describe the masks that Breton and his compatriots coveted. These native visitors to Manhattan are, in some way, treated as living, breathing artefacts; they serve as a screen onto which the imaginings of the West can be played. Yet in both cases these figures are not wholly inert: the Kwakiutl man, an informant whom Boas relied on for explanations of ethnographic material in New York museums, expresses a pointed and succinct view of his temporary American home in contrast with his northwest-coast birthplace; and the "Indian" at work in the New York Public Library makes his own notes, recording, we might imagine, his interpretation of the same marvelous cultural crossings that Lévi-Strauss records in "New York in 1941."

In his memoir, Lévi-Strauss compares himself to Alice in an American wonderland, "where anything seemed possible. Like the urban fabric, the social and cultural fabric was riddled with holes. All you had to do was pick one and slip through it, like Alice, you wanted to get to the other side of the looking glass and find worlds so enchanting that they seemed unreal" (261). But alongside this sense of endless possibility, his portrait of 1940s Manhattan conveys a premonition that this uncommon historical moment represented the beginning of an end. Clifford helps us to understand Lévi-Strauss's sense of doom by pointing out that the "delightful incongruities" and cultural variety found in New York in that era depended upon the arrival of artefacts of cultures fleeing Europe's devastation and on the "remnants of threatened or vanished traditions" destroyed by colonialism (237, 244). At its birth, then, multiculturalism presented a dual narrative: great potential, on the one hand, and apocalyptic cultural collapse, on the other.

These anecdotes help us to recognize the importance of two devastating cultural catastrophes in creating the "delightful incongruities" of wartime Manhattan: Lévi-Strauss is explicit about neither, but his enthusiasm for New York's looking-glass unreality is haunted by the aftermath of colonialism and its collecting craze, alongside an ongoing wave of desperate emigration by survivors of the Nazi Holocaust. Boas and Lévi-Strauss, both born into assimilated, Enlightenment-loving European families, do not acknowledge how their dedication to the remnants of vanishing worlds might have been influenced by a sense of their own personal losses, their distance from their ancestral homes, and, more specifically in the case of Lévi-Strauss, the Nazis' ongoing fanatical wish to make Jewish Europe the paradigm of a disappeared culture. In a perverse imitation of the anthropologist's work, German occupying forces went about collecting a great storehouse of objects that were to be used in a museum to the "preserved customs and stories" of a dead culture, to be erected in a Prague empty of Jews.

Boas's and Lévi-Strauss's fascinations mirror the narratives that have proved central to the output of post-war Jewish Canadian and American writers. We find in these writers' work a similar need to confront a dual narrative pointing to the potential of marvellous cultural crossings, made forever melancholy by a catastrophic sense of loss. Lévi-Strauss, in a recent article describing his return to the Brazilian Amazon, where he began his youthful fieldwork with the

Nambikwara, further emphasizes the centrality of such melancholy narratives to the modern imagination. In a tone reminiscent of Simon Schama's bitter-sweet afternoon spent excavating a hillside at Punsk, Lévi-Strauss considers his youthful dedication to preserving tribal cultures "menaced by Western expansion" in light of the Amazon's ongoing degradation:

At the mouth of the Amazon, the island of Marajo, 500,000 square kilometers in area, reveals a multitude of artificial hills, each occupying up to several hectares. They are man-made, erected for defense and to protect the inhabitants and cultivated fields from flooding. On the lower Amazon, remains have been unearthed of cities where, apparently, several tens of thousands of people once lived, as well as traces of unbaked bricks, substantial fortified constructions, and a network of roads leading to distant regions. ("Saudades" 20)

Lévi-Strauss's tone of wonder as he contemplates the discovery of these now-buried cities reminds us of Schama's enthusiasm at mowing through wild flower and grizzled stone to undercover a buried Jewish world. But like Schama's scenario, Lévi-Strauss's is haunted by the memory of the terrible success of European exterminatory policy: "It is often said that imported diseases, more than massacres, were responsible for the demographic collapse that followed discovery. This may be true in many cases, but it cannot erase the fact that, from the Atlantic to the Amazon, the Portuguese committed a monstrous genocide. It began in the sixteenth century and continued uninterrupted" (20).

Here we uncover a startling crossing place between a multicultural tradition that understands contemporary life as being entangled with the aftermath of colonialism and one that sees its narratives of loss and recovery through the prism of Jewish identity. In the prologue of the journal for his first voyage, Columbus celebrates what was for Spain a double triumph: "in this present year 1492 ... Your Highnesses, as Catholic Christians ... resolved to send me, Cristopher Columbus, to the said regions of India ... So then, after having expelled all the Jews from all your kingdoms and domains, in the same month of January, Your Highnesses commanded me to take sufficient ships and sail to the said regions of India" (3).[1]

In this much-documented historical moment, which includes Europe's movement outward to what would become known as the Americas, as well as the project of internal "cleansing" of those deemed parasitical on the host culture, we find a narrative of surprising juxtaposition and connection, a transcultural drama that draws together the fate of the rabbis of Seville – as they were forced east toward Polish forests and Lithuanian riverways – and the Nambikwara of the savannahs of central Brazil. The spring of 1492 sets in motion two historical narratives that ultimately lead to genocide, in which racial "cleansing" is the key motif, and buried cities – whether Amazonian or Jewish – are the conclusive outcome. We can not dismiss, then, the nostalgia of the anthropologist who dreams of his early fieldwork, or that of the historian returned to his ancestral town, as each mourns a great civilization of which only bare artefacts and markings remain. The disciplinary protocol of the social scientist usually disallows such flights of fantasy and nostalgia. So we rely on our fiction makers and poets to imagine genealogies of buried ancestry and to uncover surprising characters – miraculous, trailing wisps of cobweb and nightshadow – who maintain an uneasy balance between the demands of the present and the inheritance of the past.

Notes

1 In Calgary the architects working during the city's boom years chose modernism's mirrored façades to replace the brick and sandstone blocks that had been discredited as Old World monuments with little relationship to local mythologies. Glass towers, the eventual replacement for these monuments, were thought to "reveal the truth of the modern world to those who lived in it"; and in Calgary the truth of the modern world might be traced back to the oil find at Leduc no. 1, which initiated the areas's unprecedented growth in the post-war years (Muschamp 27). The icons of industry, progress, and technological development became so close to the heart of Canadian architects that one devoted a 1937 article, published in the Royal Architectural Institute *Journal*, to a celebration of "Gasoline Stations," praising the automobile and going on to enthuse about the "romantic" qualities of certain Canadian Tire "pit stops" (Bernstein and Cawker 11).

2 See photos numbered 51–63 and 232 in Woodall and Watkins's *Taken by the Wind*.

3 After Lazarus Cohen left Hirsch, the settlers wrote to him in Yiddish: "You know what we have – or to put it better – what we don't have. You know everything and we have nothing more to say. All we want to say and plead is: Do not forget in Montreal your brothers in Hirsch! Do not forget that more than forty families are praying daily

for you and we call your name as our saviour and protector"
(Arnold, "Life" 62).

4 On a recent visit to the Hoffer vault, I discovered the Mandels' portrait of it to be a fiction, another imagined monument to the ephemer-
ality of history. I was told by Usher Berger, on whose property the
vault stands, that when the Mandels came to visit the structure,
which once acted as a safe for the profits from local businesses but
never as an archive, it looked as it did when I found it – full of nothing but loose board, twigs, and newspaper scraps, its concrete walls
stripped of their wooden panelling.

5 Meditation upon motifs of brokenness and loss plays an important
role in Jewish traditions of mourning: "The rent garment and broken
artifacts of daily life have long served as communal signs of mourning ... Tombstone reliefs of broken candlesticks, or a splintered tree,
or a bridge half torn away, are among several repeating images recalling life interrupted by death" (Young, *Texture* 119, 186).

6 Definitions of postmodernism proliferate like the leaves in spring.
Umberto Eco, however, offers one that is relevant to the context of
this essay: "The postmodern reply to the modern consists of recognizing that the past, since it cannot really be destroyed, because its
destruction leads to silence, must be revisited: but with irony, not
innocently" (Eco 67).

7 In the plans for a condominium to be built on Vancouver's English
Bay, Henriquez includes the footprint of the apartment building that
stood on the site and of the houses that preceded it, and the first-
growth forest that predated the beach houses is referred to by concrete cast stumps set into the yard (Shubert 59).

8 Without commenting on it in poem or note, Mandel includes at the end
of *Out of Place* a letter from a representative of the Jewish Colonization
Association in London to a Canadian member of Parliament suggesting
that the site of the cemetery at Hirsch be marked. Beside the letter is
Ann Mandel's photograph of the cemetery gates (69). A plaque is in
place at the cemetery today which reads: "Hirsch Colony 1892–1942.
Erected in Commemoration of the Baron de Hirsch Jewish Agricultural
Colony. Jewish Immigrants who mostly came from Czarist Russia, Rou-
mania, Austria and Poland were assisted by the Baron de Hirsch Colonization Association. These Colonists were motivated by a keen desire to
escape religious persecution and racial discrimination, with the rights
to own and farm their land and freely adhere to their orthodox faith."

CHAPTER TWO

1 Among the many documented abuses by the Nazis of the bodies of their Jewish victims (hair for felt footwear, ash to mark pathways, gold teeth as booty pure and simple), the reported use of human fat for the production of soap is not verified by all historians. Raul Hilberg writes, in his classic study *The Destruction of the European Jews*, that the "use of human fat for soap cannot be established as a fact from available documentary evidence and eyewitness reports" (614n). He does note the prevalence of such rumours in Poland and Slovakia throughout 1942 (331, 470), as well as the testimony of a post-war mayor of Danzig, who reported that at the Stutthof camp near Danzig he "found a cauldron with the remains of boiled human flesh, a box of prepared human bones, and baskets of hands and feet and human skin, with the fat removed" (624n).

2 Primo Levi singles out Liliana Cavani's *The Night Porter* for criticism as a "beautiful and false film" that blurred the line between perpetrator and victim, while suggesting, in Cavani's words, that the "victim-executioner dynamism" exhibited by Nazis and Jews exists "in every environment, in every relationship" (*Drowned* 48). See chapter 9, where I discuss Levi's criticism of this film.

CHAPTER THREE

1 "The Holocaust and After" first appeared in 1964.

2 The *Guardian Weekly* recently reported a related controversy concerning the withdrawal of a German educational text entitled *Hitler*, which depicts the Nazi rise to power in cartoon figures. Educational authorities re-evaluated the usefulness of such a book when they considered that there

was a risk that when they read this strip cartoon pupils might identify with Hitler and pity not the victims but the murderers ...

The draughtsmanship has a well-finished quality that doesn't square with the horrors it is intended to depict. Moreover, there's not enough distance from the subject. I'm afraid some young people may take what Hitler says in a literal sense, without being able to stand back and see it in perspective. ("Hitler")

3 Richler himself was in Germany on a journalistic assignment in 1963 ("Holocaust" 88).

CHAPTER FOUR

1 The Zuckerman Trilogy – *The Ghost Writer, Zuckerman Unbound*, and *The Anatomy Lesson* – appeared with *The Prague Orgy* in 1985, under the title *Zuckerman Bound: A Trilogy and Epilogue*. My references will be to this collected volume, cited in this chapter as *ZB*.

2 *Cinnamon Shops* appeared under its original title in an English translation in 1963, which was published in London by Macgibbon & Kee.

3 Josef Skvorecky informs me that this scenario of a "gentile friend" hiding a Jewish writer in a bathroom is also true to wartime life in Prague. According to Skvorecky, the case of the hidden man is based upon the "actual life of Jiri Weil, an excellent modern Czech Jewish writer, who actually hid for a considerable time in the house of an architect friend on the corner of Wenceslas Square and Vodickova Street. The architect built a partition in the huge 19th century bathroom with his own hands and covered the entry with a mirror. Whenever the doorbell rang, Weil had to climb through the mirror, as it were."

CHAPTER FIVE

1 Attacks on Roth's artistic integrity and his relationship to Jewish culture have become a genre all their own. The most extreme among these was a letter written to *Commentary* in 1973 concerning *Portnoy's Complaint*, in which Marie Syrkin argued that Roth's work exhibited a "pathology of anti-Semitism."

2 Jauss's approach insists that instead of textual exegesis or "close reading" the task of interpretation should be to "reconstruct the historical process in which readers have received and interpreted the text at different times and in varying ways" (*Aesthetic* xxix–xxx).

3 I will denote the critical edition of the diary with the abbreviation CE. To refer to all of Anne Frank's writings I will use the term "the diary," whereas certain published selections will be referred to by their published titles, such as *Anne Frank: The Diary of a Young Girl* (as *Het Achterhuis* was called when it appeared in America in 1952). In referencing these texts I will denote *The Diary of a Young Girl* (the 1967 edition) as *Diary*.

4 This committee of judgment may be modelled after the committee that Levin appointed in an effort to avoid further legal entanglement with Otto Frank. His chosen three were novelist Charles Angoff,

Professor A. Katsch of New York University, and Rabbi Joachim
Prinz, then president of the American Jewish Congress (*Anne*, pref. ix)

5 The intricacies of what Lawrence Graver calls Levin's "fixation" with
the diary, as well as Levin's personal entanglements with Otto Frank,
are detailed in Graver's *An Obsession With Anne Frank: Meyer Levin
and the Diary*. Graver also offers a detailed discussion of Levin's "con-
tributions over a thirty-year period to an understanding of Anne
Frank's Diary and its connections to the Holocaust" (239).

6 This opinion is echoed by Ballif, who asserts, "The plot literally thick-
ens with misrepresentations" (466).

7 In Otto Frank's case, this is supported by a letter that Frank sent to
Levin in 1952: "As to the Jewish side you are right that I do not feel
the same way you do. I always said that Anne's book is not a war-
book. War is the background. It is not a Jewish book either, though
Jewish sphere, sentiment and surrounding is the background … It is
read and understood more by gentiles than in Jewish circles. So do
not make a Jewish play of it"(Doneson 152).

8 Levin readapted the events surrounding his involvement with the
diary in his novel *The Fanatic*.

9 In a forum discussing *Schindler's List* and related issues, James Young
said of the U.S. Holocaust Memorial Museum: "I was one who
wished it wouldn't be built because I was desperately afraid that this
would become all that a Jewish American community would begin
to know of itself, reducing a thousand years of European civilization
to 12 terrible years." And of *Schindler's List*: "I hope that the great
numbers that are going to see it will have their curiosity piqued
about what was lost. But I fear that they will come away sated now
that they have seen the last word on the Holocaust" ("Schindler's"
25).

   The film-maker Claude Lanzmann has written, "I wonder about
another thing, this fashion – for it really is a fashion launched by the
Americans and Israelis – for 'the just'" (14).

10 The critical edition describes Miep Gries gathering up Anne's writing
after the Franks' arrest (24) and her return of these writings to Otto
Frank when he came back to Amsterdam in June 1945 (62).

11 The critical edition of the diary describes at length the variety of writings by Anne, as well as the later production of typescripts and cop-
ies. Roth's reference to "a diary, some ledgers … and a sheaf of
papers" is basically true to the material state of her work. She wrote
initially in an autograph album given to her on her thirteenth

birthday (*ce* 59), as well as on ledger paper supplied by the Franks' protectors from the building's office supplies (24). In addition, Anne began rewriting her first diary on loose sheets, rearranging sections, combining entries, expanding and abbreviating scenes, and changing the names of her eight characters (59–62).

12 Otto Frank's gathering of carefully chosen and edited diary entries, along with some of what Anne called her "Tales and Events from the House Behind," make up the basic text that became *Het Achterhuis*, which was brought out by Amsterdam's Contact Press in the summer of 1947 (CE 71).

CHAPTER SIX

1 The novel appeared first in Yiddish in three volumes from The Menorah Press in Tel Aviv (1972). The somewhat altered version that appeared in 1985 was published in Melbourne.

2 Adam Fuerstenberg writes: "What has largely been ignored is the influence on Klein of the secular Jewish milieu which surrounded him during his formative and mature years as a creative artist and important Jewish communal figure in Montreal. This secular influence reached him mainly through Yiddish – through its modern literature and its folk traditions, both of which he knew intimately and loved – and through the institutions of Montreal's growing Jewish community as it was changing from a pioneering backwater into one of the important Yiddish centres in the world" (66).

3 Young reminds us that Thomas makes use of an account recorded, not by an eyewitness, but by the Russian writer Anatoly Kuznetsov, who relied on the testimony of Dina Pronicheva, a young woman who survived Babi Yar ("Historical" 204).

4 It is this spectacle of human frailty and fallibility that Leslie Epstein focuses on in his treatment of Rumkowski in the novel *King of the Jews*. He stages ghetto scenes that read like slapstick sketches or bits of Tin Pan Alley vaudeville. There are numerous mock-heroic scenes in which the novel's Rumkowski figure – Epstein names him Trumpelman – appears in the nick of time, bullets bouncing off him (82). The novel's concluding scene includes a Hollywood-style car chase as well as an armed rebellion unlike anything staged in Lodz. Its representation of the extremity of life in the ghetto is pushed – as experience is in vaudeville – to the extreme: people are shaken upside down, kicked, die, and return from oblivion. Even Epstein's

narrative voice mimics the winking excess of a borscht-belt comic, with its repeated use of the showman's jargon: "And that, ladies and gentlemen, is how they killed the rich Jews in our town" (72).

Epstein's choice of a slapstick ethos for his material is objectionable on the grounds that such entertainments are wholeheartedly counter-ethical (by this I do not necessarily mean unethical), in that vaudeville and slapstick motifs present a world in which no real harm is ever done, insults are borne with aplomb, and violence is a kind of manic struggle between wits.

It is worth adding, however, that Epstein chooses what can be characterized as an American Jewish tradition – that of Broadway and Hollywood kitsch – to address a Jewish catastrophe. In this way he draws on the Jewish tradition in which he has experience (he grew up in Hollywood, where his father was a screenwriter).

5 Though for Rosenfarb this word connotes paleness and ill health, it conjures as well the image of an hourglass, which was used to signify a funeral ("Klepsydra").

6 An official ghetto archive strove throughout the war to record the community's existence. The archivists wrote the *Daily Chronicle*, from which Adelson and Lapides draw some of their material, as well as the fragmentary "Encyclopedia of the Ghetto." These documents were preserved because of the swift German retreat from Lodz in 1945 (Adelson 507).

7 In some ways the transcriber's note included here is more evocative of the awful scene being depicted than Rumkowski's oratory. This notation of an upwelling of sorrow has for me the uncanny ability to conjure up the real suffering of the ghetto's inhabitants.

8 Rosenfarb touches on a number of historical events that are also noted in the records and diaries included in the Adelson and Lapides collection. Among these are a violent carpenters' strike, the emptying of the ghetto hospitals by the Nazis, the violence of the Jewish police during the deportation "actions," and the short period of hiding near the war's end from which a few survivors emerged to greet Soviet tanks.

9 Shayevitsh's long poem relies on intertextual strategies like those that I have traced in Roth's responses to the Holocaust. In David Roskies's appraisal, *Lekh-Lekho* represents a "creative use of traditional concepts such as exile and martyrdom" together with a "midrash of the moderns," a reconsideration of traditional faith through the interpretations of such poets as H. Leivick and Chaim Nachman Bialik (217).

The title of Shayevitsh's poem refers to the chapter in Exodus where Abraham is told: "Get thee out of thy country, and from thy kindred, and from thy father's house, unto the land that I will show thee. And I will make of thee a great nation, and I will bless thee" (12:1–3).

10 The translations of the sections from *Der Boim fun Lebn* that do not appear in its English translation are my own.

CHAPTER SEVEN

1 Of the studies devoted to West, the following represent only a portion of those that deal at some length with his fiction in the context of apocalyptic writing: Lewis, "Days of Wrath and Laughter"; Alter, "The Apocalyptic Temper"; Martin, *Nathanael West: The Art of His Life*; Long, *Nathanael West*; Lewicki, *The Bang and the Whimper*; and May, *Toward a New Earth*. Bloom reads *Miss Lonelyhearts* as a daemonic vision in *The Breaking of the Vessels*. Bibliographies of criticism devoted to West list a considerable number of additional titles.

2 *Miss Lonelyhearts* is cited in this chapter as *Miss* and *The Day of the Locust* as *Day*. The former appeared in 1933, and *The Day of the Locust* was published in 1939, but page references are to the edition issued in 1962, which presented the two novels in one volume.

3 Eliot's use of these symbols is particularly relevant to West's work in light of Jay Martin's assertion that West "read Eliot all through the twenties and thirties" (314). Another of Eliot's early rose-laden poems which also makes use of violet as an intimation of apocalypse is "Ash Wednesday."

CHAPTER EIGHT

1 The Branch Davidians' compound was named Mount Carmel. Carmel in Hebrew means "garden," and so connotes Eden.

2 Lal's choice of words reminds us of the strong debt owed by engineers and physicists to the writers of science fiction who dream up technological feats before they are rendered facts. "The First American Moon Landing, 1823" is the title of Joseph Atterley's 1827 fantasy of an American who meets a "venerable Hindoo," who teaches him the secrets of interplanetary travel (35). Jules Verne's *From the Earth to the Moon* (1865) begins as the rambunctious leader of a group known as the Gun Club tells his comrades, "Don't be surprised if I

am about to discourse to you regarding this Queen of the Night. It is perhaps reserved for us to become the Columbuses of this unknown world" (468). (J.F. Kennedy, invoking the American destiny to sail moonward, announced, "This is a new ocean and I believe the United States must sail upon it" [Held 319].)

In Poe's 1835 hoax, "The Unparalleled Adventure of One Hans Pfaall," the hero travels moonward in a balloon. H.G. Wells's *The First Men in the Moon* (1901) correctly prophesied our contemporary efforts at hearing "electromagnetic disturbance[s]" in the surrounding galaxy as signs of extraterrestrial life (Clarke xxxiii). Science's debt to science fiction is great, as well, in the area of communications satellite technology, which first appeared in the imaginative work of Arthur C. Clarke.

It might be argued that the recent fashion for "adventure" in cyberspace has come as space travel took on a degree of scientific certainty and became connected with government expenditure rather than individual know-how.

CHAPTER NINE

1 All references to de Man's articles are from Werner Hamacher's collection of the articles, *Wartime Journalism, 1939–1943*. I will note them by their original dates of publication since this information is extremely useful in judging the historical context within which particular articles appeared. LS designates *Le Soir*, and HVL denotes *Het Vlaamsche Land*. De Man's journalism is gathered in chronological order in Hamacher's collection.

2 Here Hamacher retains de Man's choice of the lower case for the words "jew" and "expressionism." We are reminded here of Eliot's notorious typographical choices in "Burbank with a Baedeker: Bleistein with a Cigar," as well as in "Gerontion." Both Felman and Esch (whether this decision rested with them or their publishers) tend to reinstate the capital "J," which makes for clean copy but not necessarily a clear historical picture.

3 Canadian critic Deborah Esch follows this lead in her long review article of the collection *Wartime Journalism, 1939–1943*. She addresses what she calls "an ongoing journalistic narrative" that casts "'theory' as a kind of invading force on the landscape," and she criticizes certain "academic sources" who, she argues, "take 'theory' – by which they most often mean 'deconstruction' – to be a threat to

established habits of thought and what are called traditional values" (28). Like Derrida, Esch's attention to the texts of the wartime journalism is cursory, while her ability to shuttle between the critical responses and dilemmas raised regarding de Manian deconstruction is impressive in its range. The effect is a downplaying of the issues surrounding collaboration and, as well, of any straightforward examination of the responsibility of individuals or broader traditions with regard to the events of the war. The "crisis" brought about by the uncovering of de Man's wartime writings is always referred to using quotation marks, a rhetorical move which suggests that undue and dishonest work has been made of this discovery. For Esch, the attack on deconstruction and theory in the academy is the true crisis at hand.

She is fascinated as well by the fact that responses to the wartime writings were often "drawn from de Man's theoretical legacy," meaning that such responses were often de Manian in style (33). But this seems an excellent example of what Dominick LaCapra calls transference – the tendency unconsciously to reproduce the object of one's study, rather than to critique it adequately. Esch's article undertakes a detailed reading of de Man's influential work on Husserl, Goethe, Schiller, and Kleist, to point to how his willingness to read texts for points of rhetorical "blindness" should help redress the "pattern of self-mystification inscribed in the wartime writings" (35).

4 In his 1993 study *Serenity in Crisis: A Preface to Paul de Man, 1939–1960*, Ortwin de Graef resurrects this questionable approach, noting de Man's youthful enthusiasms to account for what de Graef suggests is the sophisticated, implicitly deconstructive nature of the wartime journalist's project:

a reasonably successful student of science with an evident interest in literature and in ideological issues abandons a scientific career, inconclusively turns to social sciences, and ends up as literary reviewer. The pattern involves three practices – the discourse of natural science, of social science, and of literature – and it quasi-mechanically invites the hypothesis that it is in the contest of these faculties that de Man's early work comes to be written, in an awareness of the rivaling claims to truth represented by these three disciplines ... It may seem far-fetched to read such an ambitious and prestigious desire to police the disciplines in pieces of journalism which at first sight could so much more economically be explained as the hack work of a young opportunist, but as I shall try to show, this desire is arguably one of their main formative concerns. (6)

5 This urge to distinguish between "vulgar" and "polite" anti-Semitism raises an unpleasant echo of the discourse common in right-wing French intellectual and political circles during and since the war. In a 1982 interview with Maurice Bardèche – an editor of the extreme right review *Défense de l'occident* as well as of Flaubert and Proust – Alice Kaplan records Bardèche's justification of what he calls the "anti-Semitism of reason." According to him, this reasoned, polite anti-Semitism, which was felt by "a great part of the French," was based on the desire to "limit the Jewish influence in France" (*Reproductions* 173).

CONCLUSION

1 An edict signed by Ferdinand and Isabella on 30 March 1492 required all Jews either to convert to Christianity or to leave the country by midnight on 2 August of that year. On 17 April 1492 the letters authorizing Columbus's voyage were signed.

Bibliography

Abbott, Jack. *In the Belly of the Beast: Letters from Prison*. New York: Random House, 1981.

Adelson, Alan, and R. Lapides, eds. *Łódź Ghetto: Inside a Community under Siege*. New York: Viking, 1989.

Alter, Robert. "The Apocalyptic Temper." *Commentary* 41 (1966): 61–6.

– and F. Kermode., eds. *The Literary Guide to the Bible*. Cambridge: Harvard University Press, 1987.

Anne Frank in the World / De Werlde van Anne Frank. Amsterdam: Uitgenerij Bert Baker, 1985.

"Apocalypse." *The Encyclopaedia Judaica*. 1971 ed.

Arendt, Hannah. Introduction. *Auschwitz: A Report*. Ed. Bernd. Naumann. xi–xxx.

Arnold, A.J. "Jewish Immigration to Western Canada in the 1880's." *Canadian Jewish Historical Society Journal* 1 (1977): 82–96.

– "Jewish Pioneer Settlements." *Beaver* 306.2 (1975): 20–9.

– "The Life and Times of Jewish Pioneers in Western Canada." *The Jewish Historical Society of Western Canada Second Annual Publication: A Selection of Papers Presented in 1969–70. 51–77.

Atterley, Joseph. "The First American Moon Landing, 1823." *Michigan Quarterly Review* 18 (1979): 355–63.

Atwood, Margaret. *Survival*. Toronto: Anansi, 1972.

Baird, James. *Ishmael: A Study of the Symbolic Mode in Primitivism*. New York: Harper, 1956.

Ballif, Algene. "Anne Frank on Broadway: Metamorphosis into American Adolescent." Rev. of *The Diary of Anne Frank*, by F. Goodrich and A. Hackett. *Commentary* Nov. 1955: 464–7.

Barron, Stephanie, et al. *"Degenerate Art": The Fate of the Avant-Garde in Nazi Germany.* New York: Abrams, 1991.

Beatty, Jack. Rev. of *The Ghost Writer*, by Philip Roth. *New Republic* 6 Oct. 1979: 36–40.

Bellow, Saul. *The Bellarosa Connection.* New York: Penguin, 1989.

– *Mr. Sammler's Planet.* 1970. New York: Penguin, 1977.

Bergaust, Eric. *Wernher von Braun.* Washington: National Space Institute, 1976.

Bernasconi, R., and D. Wood, eds. *The Provocation of Levinas: Rethinking the Other.* New York: Routledge, 1988.

Bernstein, Michael André. *Foregone Conclusions: Against Apocalyptic History.* Berkeley: University of California Press, 1994.

Bernstein, W., and R. Cawker. *Building with Words: Canadian Architects on Architecture.* Toronto: Coach House, 1981.

Bettelheim, Bruno. "The Ignored Lesson of Anne Frank." *Surviving and Other Essays.* 1952. New York: Vintage, 1980. 246–57.

Blanchot, Maurice. "Literary Infinity: The Aleph." *The Sirens' Song: Selected Essays.* Ed. G. Josipivici. Trans. S. Rabinovitch. Bloomington: Indiana University Press, 1982. 222–4.

Bloom, Harold. *The Breaking of the Vessels.* Chicago: University of Chicago Press, 1982.

Boyarin, Daniel. *Intertextuality and the Reading of Midrash.* Bloomington: Indiana University Press, 1990.

– and Jonathan Boyarin. "Diaspora: Generation and the Ground of Jewish Identity." *Critical Inquiry* 19 (1993): 693–725.

Brydon, Diana. "Reading Postcoloniality, Reading Canada." *Essays on Canadian Writing* 56 (1995): 1–19.

Buber, Martin. "Prophecy, Apocalyptic, and the Historical Hour." *Biblical Humanism: Eighteen Studies.* Ed. N. Glatzer. London: Macdonald, 1968. 172–87.

Burroughs, William. *Naked Lunch.* New York: Grove, 1959.

Clarke, A.C. Introduction. *The First Men in the Moon.* By H.G. Wells. London: Dent, 1993. xxix–xxxiv.

Clifford, James. *The Predicament of Culture: Twentieth-Century Ethnography, Literature, and Art.* Cambridge: Harvard University Press, 1988.

Cohen, Leonard. *Beautiful Losers.* 1966. Toronto: McClelland and Stewart, 1986.

– *The Favourite Game.* 1963. Toronto: McClelland and Stewart, 1970

Collins, John. "Apocalyptic Eschatology as the Transcendence of Death." *Catholic Biblical Quarterly* 36 (1974): 21–43.

– "Towards the Morphology of a Genre." *Semeia* 14.1 (1979): 1–20.

Columbus, Christopher. *Journal of the First Voyage*. Trans & ed. B.W. Ife. Warminster: Aris & Phillips, 1990.

Cook, Eleanor. "The Decreations of Wallace Stevens." *Wallace Stevens Journal* 4 (1980): 46–57.

– *Poetry, Word-Play, and Word-War in Wallace Stevens*. Princeton: Princeton University Press, 1988.

de Graef, Ortwin. *Serenity in Crisis: A Preface to Paul de Man 1939–1960*. Lincoln: University of Nebraska Press, 1993.

– "Silence to Be Observed: A Trial for Paul de Man's Inexcusable Confessions." *(Dis)continuities*. Ed. L. Herman et al. 51–73.

Derrida, Jacques. "Like the Sound of the Sea Deep within a Shell: Paul de Man's War." *Responses*. Ed. Werner Hamacher et al. 127–64.

– "Of an Apocalyptic Tone Recently Adopted in Philosophy." *Semeia* 23 (1982): 63–97.

Doneson, Judith. "The American History of Anne Frank's Diary." *Holocaust and Genocide Studies* 2.1 (1987): 149–60.

Dostoyevsky, Fyodor. *The Brothers Karamozov*. Trans. C. Garnett. New York: The Modern Library, n.d.

Eco, Umberto. *Postscript to the Name of the Rose*. New York: Harcourt Brace Jovanovich, 1984.

Eliot, T.S. *Collected Poems, 1909–1962*. London: Faber, 1983.

Epstein, Leslie. *King of the Jews*. New York: Coward, McCann & Geoghegan, 1979.

Esch, Deborah. "The Work to Come." *diacritics* 20.3 (1990): 28–49.

Felman, Shoshana. "After the Apocalypse: Paul de Man and the Fall to Silence." *Testimony*. Ed. Shoshana Felman and Dori Laub. 120–64.

– "Paul de Man's Silence." *Critical Inquiry* 15 (1989): 704–44.

– and Dori Laub. *Testimony: Crises of Witnessing in Literature, Psychoanalysis, and History*. New York: Routledge, 1992.

Ficowski, J. Introduction. *The Street of Crocodiles*. By Bruno Schulz. New York: Penguin, 1977. 13–22.

–, ed. *Letters and Drawings of Bruno Schulz*. Trans. W. Arndt. New York: Harper and Row, 1988.

Fiedler, Leslie. *The Return of the Vanishing American*. New York: Stein and Day, 1968.

Finkielkraut, Alain. *The Imaginary Jew*. 1980. Trans. K. O'Neill and D. Suchoff. Lincoln: University of Nebraska Press, 1994.

Frank, Anne. *The Diary of a Young Girl*. 1952. Trans. B.M. Mooyaart-Doubleday. New York: Doubleday, 1967.

– *The Diary of Anne Frank: The Critical Edition*. Ed. D. Barnouw and G. Van der Stroom. Trans. A.J. Pomerans et al. Introd. H. Paape, G. Van der Stroom, and D. Barnouw. New York: Doubleday, 1989. Cited as CE in the text.

Friedlander, Saul, ed. Introduction. *Probing the Limits of Representation: Nazism and the "Final Solution."* Cambridge: Harvard University Press, 1992.

– *Reflections of Nazism: An Essay on Kitsch and Death*. 1982. Trans. T. Weyr. New York: Harper & Row, 1984.

– *When Memory Comes*. 1978. Trans. H. Lane. New York: Farrar Strauss Giroux, 1979.

Frye, Northrop. *Anatomy of Criticism: Four Essays*. Princeton: Princeton University Press, 1957.

Fuerstenberg, Adam. "From Yiddish to 'Yiddishkeit': A.M. Klein, J.I. Segal and Montreal's Yiddish Culture." *Journal of Canadian Studies* 19 (1984): 66–81.

Ginsberg, Allen. *Howl, and Other Poems*. San Francisco: City Lights, 1959.

Golsan, R. "Ideology, Cultural Politics and Literary Collaboration at *La Gerbe.*" *Journal of European Studies*. 23 (1993): 27–47.

Goodrich, Frances, and Albert Hackett. *The Diary of Anne Frank*. New York: Random House, 1956.

Gourevitch, Philip. "After the Genocide." *New Yorker* 18 Dec. 1995: 78–95.

Grace, S. *Regression and Apocalypse: Studies in North American Literary Expressionism*. Toronto: University of Toronto Press, 1989.

Graver, Lawrence. *An Obsession with Anne Frank: Meyer Levin and the Diary*. Berkeley: University of California Press, 1995.

Greenblatt, Stephen. *Learning to Curse: Essays in Early Modern Culture*. New York: Routledge, 1990.

– ed. Introduction. *Representing the English Renaissance*. Berkeley: University of California Press, 1988.

Greenstein, Michael. *Third Solitudes: Tradition and Discontinuity in Jewish-Canadian Literature*. Kingston: McGill-Queen's University Press, 1989.

Hamacher, Werner, et al., eds. *Responses: On Paul de Man's Wartime Journalism*. Lincoln: University of Nebraska Press, 1989.

– *Wartime Journalism, 1939–1943*. By Paul de Man. Lincoln: University of Nebraska Press, 1988.

Harbison, Robert. *The Built, the Unbuilt and the Unbuildable: In Pursuit of Architectural Meaning*. London: Thames and Hudson, 1991.

Harpham, G.G. *On the Grotesque: Strategies of Contradiction in Art and Literature.* Princeton: Princeton University Press, 1982.

Hartman, Geoffrey. "Blindness and Insight." *New Republic* 7 March 1988: 26–31.

Held, George. "Men on the Moon: American Novelists Explore Lunar Space." *Michigan Quarterly Review* 18 (1979): 318–42.

Herman, L., et al., eds. *(Dis)continuities: Essays on Paul de Man.* Amsterdam: Rodopi, 1989.

Hilberg, Raul. *The Destruction of the European Jews.* Chicago: Quadrangle, 1961.

– "I Was Not There." *Writing and the Holocaust.* Ed. Berel Lang. 17–25.

"Hirsch, Baron Maurice de." *Encyclopaedia Judaica.* 1971 ed.

"Hitler Strip Cartoon Sparks Schools Row." *Guardian Weekly* 7 Nov. 1993: 14.

Holocaust. Writ. Gerald Green. NBC. 1978.

The Holy Bible. King James Version. New York: American Bible Society, 1968.

Hutcheon, Linda. *Leonard Cohen and His Works.* Toronto: ECWP, 1989.

Hyman, Stanley E. "Nathanael West." *Twentieth Century Interpretations of Miss Lonelyhearts.* Ed. T.H. Jackson. Englewood Cliffs: Prentice-Hall, 1971. 70–80.

Jakobson, R. "Boas' View of Grammatical Meaning." *The Anthropology of Franz Boas.* Ed. W. Goldschmidt. San Francisco: American Anthropological Association, 1959. 139–45.

Jauss, Hans. *Aesthetic Experience and Literary Hermeneutics.* 1977. Trans. M. Shaw. Minneapolis: University of Minnesota Press, 1982.

– "An Interview with Hans Robert Jauss." *New Literary History* 11 (1979): 83–95.

Kafka, Franz. *Letter to His Father / Brief an Den Vater.* Trans. E. Kaiser and E. Wilkins. New York: Schocken, 1966.

Kamboureli, Smaro. "Locality as Writing: A Preface to the 'Preface' of *Out of Place.*" *Open Letter* 6 (1985): 267–77.

Kaplan, Alice. *French Lessons: A Memoir.* Chicago: University of Chicago Press, 1993.

– *Reproductions of Banality: Fascism, Literature, and French Intellectual Life.* Minneapolis: University of Minnesota Press, 1986.

Kayser, Wolfgang. *The Grotesque in Art and Literature.* Trans. U. Weisstein. New York: Columbia University Press, 1957.

Kellen, Konrad. "*Seven Beauties*: Auschwitz – The Ultimate Joke?" *Midstream* Oct. 1976: 59–66.

Kermode, F. "Paul de Man's Abyss." *The Uses of Error.* London: Collins, 1990. 102–18.

– *The Sense of an Ending: Studies in the Theory of Fiction*. London: Oxford, 1967.

– and Robert Alter, eds. *The Literary Guide to the Bible*. Cambridge: Harvard University Press, 1987.

Kerouac, Jack. *On the Road*. New York: Viking, 1959.

Kershaw, Ian. *The "Hitler Myth": Image and Reality in the Third Reich*. Oxford: Clarendon, 1987.

– *The Nazi Dictatorship: Problems and Perspectives of Interpretation*. 2nd ed. London: Arnold, 1989.

Klein, A.M. *The Second Scroll*. 1951. Toronto: McClelland & Stewart, 1969.

"Klepsydra." *The Great Polish-English Dictionary*. 1975 ed.

Kulyk Keefer, Janice. "From Mosaic to Kaleidoscope." *Books in Canada* 20.6 (1991): 13–16.

– "Memory, Story, Text: Transcultural Aesthetics and Norman Ravvin's *Café des Westens*." Unpublished essay, 1994.

LaCapra, Dominick. "Representing the Holocaust: Reflections on the Historian's Debate." Unpublished essay, 1991.

– *Soundings in Critical Theory*. Ithaca: Cornell University Press, 1989.

– Rev. of *Why Did the Heavens Not Darken? The "Final Solution" in History*, by Arno J. Mayer. *New German Critique* 53 (1991): 175–91.

Lang, Berel, ed. *Writing and the Holocaust*. New York: Holmes & Meier, 1988.

Lanzmann, Claude. "Why Spielberg Has Distorted the Truth." *Manchester Guardian Weekly* 3 April 1994: 14.

Lee, Dennis. *Savage Fields: An Essay in Literature and Cosmology*. Toronto: Anansi, 1977.

Lee, Hermione. *Philip Roth*. New York: Methuen, 1982.

Leonoff, C.E. *The Jewish Farmers of Western Canada*. Vancouver: Jewish Historical Society of British Columbia and Western States Jewish History Association, 1984.

Levi, Primo. *The Drowned and the Saved*. 1986. Trans. R. Rosenthal. New York: Vintage, 1989.

– *Survival in Auschwitz*. 1958. Trans. S. Woolf. New York: Macmillan, 1961.

Levin, Meyer. *Anne Frank: A Play*. Privately published by Meyer Levin, 1967.

– *The Fanatic*. New York: Simon and Schuster, 1963.

– *The Obsession*. New York: Simon and Schuster, 1973.

Levinas, Emmanuel. "The Paradox of Morality." Trans. T. Wright. *The Provocation of Levinas*. Ed. R. Bernasconi and D. Wood. 169–80.

– "Signature." *Difficult Freedom: Essays on Judaism*. Trans. S. Hand. London: Athlone, 1990. 291–5.

– "Useless Suffering." *The Provocation of Levinas*. Ed. R. Bernasconi and D. Wood. 156–67.

Lévi-Strauss, Claude. "New York in 1941." *The View from Afar*. Trans. J. Neugroschel. New York: Basic, 1985. 258–67.

– "Saudades do Brasil." *New York Review of Books* 21 Dec. 1995: 19–26.

Lewicki, Z. *The Bang and the Whimper: Apocalypse and Entropy in American Literature*. Westport: Greenwood, 1984.

Lewis, R.W.B. "Days of Wrath and Laughter." *Trials of the Word: Essays in American Literature and the Humanistic Tradition*. New Haven: Yale University Press, 1965. 184–235.

Light, James. *Nathanael West: An Interpretive Study*. 2nd ed. Evanston: Northwestern University Press, 1971.

Liptzin, Sol. *A History of Yiddish Literature*. New York: Jonathan David, 1972.

Locklin, G. "The Man Behind the Novels." *Nathanael West: The Cheaters and the Cheated*. Ed. David Madden. Deland: Everett/Edwards, 1973. 1–15.

Long, R.E. *Nathanael West*. New York: Ungar, 1985.

McGinn, Bernard. "Revelation." *The Literary Guide to the Bible*. Ed. F. Kermode and Robert Alter. 523–41.

Mailer, Norman. *The Executioner's Song*. Boston: Little, Brown, 1979.

Maloff, Saul. "The Uses of Adversity." Rev. of *The Ghost Writer*, by Philip Roth. *Commonweal* 9 Nov. 1979: 628–31.

Mandel, Eli. "Auschwitz: Poetry of Alienation." *Canadian Literature* 100 (1984): 213–18.

– "Earthworms Eat Earthworms and Learn." *Stony Plain*. 54–5.

– "Interview with Eli Mandel, March 16/78." By David Arnason et al. *Essays on Canadian Writing* 118/19 (1980): 70–90.

– "Leonard Cohen." *The Family Romance*. Winnipeg: Turnstone, 1986. 207–11.

– *Out of Place*. Erin: Press Porcépic, 1977.

– *Stony Plain*. Erin: Press Porcépic, 1973.

Martin, Jay. *Nathanael West: The Art of His Life*. New York: Farrar, 1970.

May, John R. *Toward a New Earth: Apocalypse in the American Novel*. Notre Dame, Ind.: University of Notre Dame Press, 1972.

Mehlman, Jeffrey. *Legacies of Anti-Semitism in France*. Minneapolis: University of Minnesota Press, 1983.

Meisler, Stanley. "The World of Bosch." *Smithsonian* 18 (1988): 40–55.

Mosse, George L. *Germans and Jews: the Right, the Left, and the Search for a "Third Force" in Pre-Nazi Germany*. New York: Howard Fertig, 1970.

– "Hitler Redux." *New Republic* 16 June 1979: 21–4.

Muschamp, H. "How Buildings Remember." *New Republic* 28 Aug. 1989: 27–33.

Naumann, Bernd., ed. *Auschwitz: A Report on the Proceedings against Robert Karl Ludwig Mulka and Others before the Court at Frankfurt*. Trans. J. Steinberg. New York: Prager, 1966.

The New Oxford Annotated Bible with the Apocrypha. Revised Standard Edition. 1977.

O'Brien, Conor Cruise. *On the Eve of the Millennium*. Toronto: Anansi, 1994.

Olson, Charles. *Charles Olson & Ezra Pound: An Encounter at St. Elizabeths*. Ed. C. Seelye. New York: Grossman, 1975.

Ondaatje, Michael. *Leonard Cohen*. Toronto: McClelland & Stewart, 1970.

Ozick, Cynthia. "The Street of Crocodiles: With Babel and Singer and Kafka." *New York Times Book Review* 15 Feb. 1977: 4–5.

Pagels, Elaine. "The Social History of Satan, the 'Intimate Enemy': A Preliminary Sketch." *Harvard Theological Review* 84.2 (1991): 105–28.

Parry, I. "Kafka, Gogol and Nathanael West." *Kafka: A Collection of Critical Essays*. Ed. R. Gray. Englewood Cliffs: Prentice Hall, 1962. 85–90.

Pasqualino Settebellezze [Seven Beauties]. Dir. Lina Wertmuller. 1976.

Pérez-Gómez, A. "The Architecture of Richard Henriquez: A Praxis of Personal Memory." *Richard Henriquez et le Théâtre de la mémoire*. Ed. Howard Shubert. 9–30.

Poe, Edgar Allan. "The Unparalleled Adventure of One Hans Pfaall." *The Complete Tales and Poems of Edgar Allan Poe*. New York: Random House, 1938. 3–41.

Portiere di Notte [The Night Porter]. Dir. Liliana Cavani. 1974.

Proust, Marcel. *The Captive*. Trans. G.K. Scott Moncrieff. New York: Vintage, 1971.

Richler, Mordecai. "The Holocaust and After." *Shovelling Trouble*. 84–96.

– *St. Urbain's Horseman*. 1971. New York: Bantam, 1972.

– *Shovelling Trouble*. Toronto: McClelland & Stewart, 1972.

– "Why I Write." *Shovelling Trouble*. 11–22.

Rodgers, B. *Philip Roth: A Bibliography.* 2nd ed. New Jersey: Scarecrow, 1984.

Rosenfarb, Chava. *Der Boim fun Lebn*. 3 vols. Tel Aviv: Hamenorah, 1972.

– *The Tree of Life*. Trans. C. Rosenfarb and G. Morgenthaler. Melbourne: Scribe, 1985.

"Rosenfarb, Chaveh." *The Oxford Companion to Canadian Literature*. 1972 ed.

Roskies, David. *Against the Apocalypse: Responses to Catastrophe in Modern Jewish Culture*. Cambridge: Harvard University Press, 1984.

Roth, Philip. *The Anatomy Lesson. Zuckerman Bound*. 247–420.

– *The Counterlife*. New York: Farrar, 1987.

– *The Ghost Writer. Zuckerman Bound*. 3–108. Originally published separately in 1979 by Farrar, Straus and Giroux of New York.

- "The Ghosts of Roth." Interview with A. Finkielkraut. *Conversations with Philip Roth*. Ed. G. Searles. Jackson: University Press of Mississippi, 1992. 120–30.
- "'I Always Wanted You to Admire My Fasting'; or, Looking at Kafka." *Reading Myself and Others*. 247–70.
- *Portnoy's Complaint*. New York: Random House, 1969.
- *The Prague Orgy. Zuckerman Bound*. 423–72.
- *The Professor of Desire*. New York: Farrar, Straus and Giroux, 1977.
- *Reading Myself and Others*. New York: Farrar, Straus and Giroux, 1975.
- "Roth and Singer on Bruno Schulz." Interview with I.B. Singer. *New York Times Book Review* 13 Feb. 1977: 5+.
- *Zuckerman Bound: A Trilogy and Epilogue*. New York: Fawcett, 1985. Cited as *ZB* in the text.
- *Zuckerman Unbound. Zuckerman Bound*. 111–214.
Santner, Eric. "History beyond the Pleasure Principle: Some Thoughts on the Representation of Trauma." *Probing the Limits of Representation*. Ed. Saul Friedlander. 143–54.
- *Stranded Objects: Mourning, Memory, and Film in Postwar Germany*. Ithaca: Cornell University Press, 1990.
Sartre, Jean-Paul. *What Is Literature?* Trans. Bernard Frechtman. Bristol: Methuen, 1983.
Schama, Simon. *Landscape and Memory*. Toronto: Random House, 1995.
Schindler's List. Dir. Steven Spielberg. Universal, 1994.
"Schindler's List: Myth, Movie, and Memory." *Village Voice* 29 March 1994: 24–31.
Scholem, Gershom. "On Eichmann." *Thinking the Unthinkable: Meanings of the Holocaust*. Ed. R. Gottlieb. New York: Paulist Press, 1990.
Schulz, Bruno. *Cinnamon Shops*. Trans. C. Wieniewska. London: Macgibbon, 1963.
- *The Street of Crocodiles*. Trans. C. Wieniewska. New York: Penguin, 1977.
Scobie, Stephen. *Leonard Cohen*. Vancouver: Douglas & McIntyre, 1978.
Shatzky, Joel. "Creating an Aesthetic for Holocaust Literature." *Studies in American Jewish Literature* 10 (1991): 104–14.
Shayevitsh, Simcha Bunim. *Lekh-Lekho*. Lodz: The Lodz Jewish Historical Commission, 1946.
Sheppard, R.Z. "A Tale of Tough Cookies." Rev. of *The Ghost Writer*, by Philip Roth. *Time* 3 Sept. 1979: 70.
Shubert, Howard., ed. *Richard Henriquez et le Théâtre de la mémoire / Richard Henriquez: Memory Theatre*. Vancouver: Vancouver Art Gallery, 1993.
Singer, I.B. *In My Father's Court*. New York: Farrar, 1966.

Skvorecky, Josef. Letter to the author. Undated.

Söderlind, Sylvia. *Margin/Alias: Language and Colonization in Canadian and Québécois Fiction*. Toronto: University of Toronto Press, 1991.

"Songs of Innocence and Experience." Rev. of *The Diary of Anne Frank*, by F. Goodrich and A. Hackett. *Commonweal* 28 Oct. 1959: 91–2.

Sontag, Susan. "Fascinating Fascism." *Under the Sign of Saturn*. New York: Farrar Straus Giroux, 1980. 73–105.

Steiner, George. *In Bluebeard's Castle: Some Notes towards the Re-definition of Culture*. London: Faber, 1971.

Stengers, John. "Paul de Man, a Collaborator." *(Dis)continuities*. Ed. L. Herman et al. 43–50.

Styron, William. *Sophie's Choice*. 1979. New York: Bantam, 1980.

Suleiman, Susan R. "War Memories: On Autobiographical Reading." *Auschwitz and After: Race, Culture, and "The Jewish Question" in France*. Ed. L. Kritzman. New York: Routledge, 1995. 47–62.

Syrkin, Marie. Letter. *Midstream* March 1973: 8–9.

Talmon, S. "Daniel." *The Literary Guide to the Bible*. Ed. F. Kermode and Robert Alter. 343–56.

Tennyson, Alfred, Lord. *In Memoriam*. Ed. S. Shatto and M. Shaw. Oxford: Clarendon, 1982.

Thomas, D.M. *The White Hotel*. London: Penguin, 1981.

Towers, Robert. "The Lesson of the Master." Rev. of *The Ghost* Writer, by Philip Roth. *New York Times Book Review* 2 Sept. 1979: 1+.

Verhovek, Sam. "After Bombing, a Rush to Visit Davidian Site." *New York Times* 5 May 1995: A1+.

Verne, Jules. *From the Earth to the Moon. Jules Verne: Collected Works*. Seacaucus: Castle, 1984. 463–564.

Warkentin, John. "Time and Place in the Western Interior." *artscanada* 22 (1972): 20–35.

West, Nathanael. *Miss Lonelyhearts & The Day of the Locust*. New York: New Directions, 1962.

– "Some Notes on Miss L." *Contempo* 15 May 1933: 1–2.

– "Some Notes on Violence." *Contact* 1 (1932): 132–3.

Whitman, Walt. *Leaves of Grass*. New York: Penguin, 1988.

Wieniewska, C. Preface. *The Street of Crocodiles*. By Bruno Schulz. New York: Penguin, 1977.

Wiesel, Elie. *Night*. 1958. Trans. S. Rodway. New York: Bantam, 1989.

Wieseltier, Leon. "After Memory: Reflections on the Holocaust Memorial Museum." *New Republic* 3 May 1993: 16–26.

Wilson, Matthew. "*The Ghost Writer*: Kafka, *Het Achterhuis*, and History." *Studies in American Jewish Literature* 10 (1991): 44–53.

Woodall, Ronald, and T.H. Watkins. *Taken by the Wind: Vanishing Architecture of the West*. Don Mills, Ont.: Gage, 1977.

A Worldwide Philanthropic Empire: The Life Work of Baron Maurice de Hirsch. Tel Aviv: Bet ha-tefutsot, 1982.

Young, James E. "Historical Writing and the Memory of the Holocaust." *Writing and the Holocaust*. Ed. Berel Lang. New York: Homes & Meier, 1988. 200–15.

– *The Texture of Memory: Holocaust Memorials and Meaning*. New Haven: Yale University Press, 1993.

Index